McCALL'S
Introduction to
GERMAN
COOKING

McCALL'S
Introduction to
GERMAN
COOKING

Edited by Linda Wolfe

Saturday Review Press

NEW YORK

Published simultaneously in Canada by Doubleday Canada Ltd., Toronto.

Library of Congress Catalog Card Number: 73-157911

ISBN 0-8415-0131-9

Printed in the United States of America

Design by Tere LoPrete

Saturday Review Press

230 Park Avenue, New York, New York 10017

Contents

Introduction

The German kitchen has always emphasized hearty and nourishing food, a characteristic that makes German cooking pleasantly familiar to Americans. The German cuisine is one that relies on the inherent good flavor and quality of food rather than on involved cooking procedures or complicated embellishments; a bay leaf, a pinch of marjoram, a sprig of parsley, for example, are considered ample seasoning for a sauce. Substantial soups, crusty dark breads, an infinite variety of sausages, superb marinated meat and vegetable dishes, delicious buttery cakes and cookies—these are German favorites. Such food preferences are part of a culinary tradition that goes back to the days when agriculture was the prime means of livelihood. Peasants spent long hours tilling the land and required nourishing foods to sustain them through the long work day. Today, of course, Germany is one of the world's foremost industrial nations and only a small number of people are engaged in farming. Yet, for the best of reasons, Germans still relish the robust dishes of their ancestors: They are incomparably good.

Historically, there has never been a single style of cooking in Germany, which was one of the last European countries to become unified. Throughout the Middle Ages and the Renaissance, when England, France, and Spain were already influential nations, Germany was a collection of independent, rival duchies and principalities. The different political regions spoke different dialects, observed different customs, and practiced different culinary styles that depended on local produce. In 1871, the various regions were united under Kaiser Wilhelm I, and the German nation was born. To some extent, however, three major regions remained, each having its own cuisine: one in the north of Germany, one in the center of the country, and one in the south. These regions still exist today, even though the country is now divided politically into East and West Germany.

The cooking of the northern provinces, which are bounded on the west by Holland, on the north by Scandinavia, and on the east by Poland and, beyond, Russia, reflects the influences of these countries. East of Berlin, in the region that used to be called Prussia, ingredients such as sour cream, vinegar, and smoked bacon are commonly used; regional dishes here are similar to those of the U.S.S.R. and Poland. To the north, in Schleswig-Holstein, the Scandinavian influence is apparent in the popularity of herring and pickled fish, hot and cold soups, and vegetables that store well through the cold weather, such as beets, potatoes, lentils, and split peas. In the cosmopolitan cities of Hamburg, Bremen, and Berlin, the cooking is diversified, and a more international cuisine is to be found.

It is in central Germany, a region of hills, forests, and fertile uplands and valleys, that the food that most Americans consider typically German is prepared. Dumplings, wurst or sausage, cabbage, and turnips comprise the hearty meals that are accompanied by huge steins of local beer and a glass of fiery schnapps. Much of this traditional German fare is culled from local products: pork, rye, and sugar beets and other root vegetables. Other local specialties include the smoky ham of Westphalia, the rich fruit tarts of Thuringia, and a beef sausage from Frankfurt—which Americans have adopted as their own hot dog.

In the south of Germany, the two distinctive cooking styles are the Bavarian and the lighter, more delicate cuisine of the Rhine country. Bavaria, stretching out across southern Germany, contains high plateaus well suited to the raising of wheat and of barley, the raw ingredient that stocks Germany's thousands of breweries. For centuries, Bavaria has been noted for its delights of the table. Outstanding are its game, including venison and partridge, and baked goods such as strudel and Black-Forest Cake. The region of Bavaria, and of Baden to the west, is also dotted with resorts and spas. While visitors may come especially for the healthful mineral waters, most do not leave without participating in a beer or a wine festival, for which the area is celebrated. Munich's fall Oktoberfest and the early-spring Fasching are among the most popular festivities.

Along the banks of the Rhine and Moselle rivers to the west of Bavaria, the landscape rises in steep, sun-drenched hills. This area produces Germany's renowned white wines, made from grapes from vineyards that have been cultivated since the days of the Romans. The food is simple, often consisting of one-dish meals, such as the outstanding regional specialty Himmel und Erde, a mixture of potatoes and apples, usually served with blood sausage.

Even today the produce from each area can be found at local outdoor markets, where housewives fill their baskets with farm-fresh eggs, home-baked breads, and fruits fresh from the tree. The outdoor markets are no longer as active as they once were, owing to the growth and popularity of the supermarket in German cities and towns. Today there are hundreds of modern supermarkets stocked with foods from all over the world: curry from India, truffles from France, and tropical fruits. Yet in spite of the availability of international products, traditional German foods still dominate the tables of the country.

In tracing the development of German cooking, we gain our earliest information from the Roman historian Tacitus. In his *Germania,* written in the first century A.D., he gave the Romans a colorful description of their barbaric neighbors to the north. The Romans, whose food preferences included peacocks' tongues and thick wine sauces, were astounded by the simplicity of German cooking, which was based, reported Tacitus, on "fruits, nuts, and sour milk." It is interesting to note how these culinary preferences have survived through the years. While Italians no longer dine on peacocks' tongues as they did two thousand years ago, they still make sauces with wine bases. And German cooking still relies heavily on fruits, nuts, and sour milk. Apples, for example, appear not only in German desserts, but in soups, casseroles, and meat stews; pears are baked with bacon, prunes steamed with fish. Nuts are used in German salads and dressings and in one of the best German vegetable sauces, a hazelnut butter sauce that is served on asparagus or spread on bread. Sour cream and buttermilk are often stirred into poultry and meat casseroles.

Another component of German cooking that existed in the time of Tacitus is still extremely important today: pork. In the city of Cologne, founded as a Roman outpost on the Rhine, a villa nearly two thousand years old has been unearthed. One of the mosaic floors shows a feast that features local food—including a roasted wild boar. The boar's modern counterpart, the pig, which is carefully raised to produce a fat and succulent animal, is used in the preparation of most popular German dishes. There are hundreds of pork recipes in the German cooking repertoire, as well as about three hundred different varieties of pork sausage.

During the Middle Ages and the Renaissance, the German aristocracy and wealthy merchant families emulated the culinary styles of other European countries. Like the English, they roasted meat over open fires and baked birds and fish in deep pies that were called "coffins" because the fowl or fish was buried in the pastry dough. Like the French, they cooked fish in white wine and poultry with truffles and cream sauces, and they created "show dishes" whose preparation was as elaborate and artistic as the silver, gold, and ivory tableware upon which the food was presented. Like the Italians, the Germans traded with Arab merchants for the costly and important spices from the East: saffron, cumin, cloves, coriander. The most valuable spice was pepper, which was used as a preservative and to disguise the taste of food that had begun to spoil. Indeed, pepper was so highly regarded that it became the measure of a man's wealth. Instead of being called "moneybags," successful German merchants were called *Pfeffersäcke,* or "pepperbags."

By the end of the nineteenth century, Germany was united as a nation, and the middle class had acquired power and influence in the country. Although they adopted many customs of the aristocracy, when it came to dining they favored the robust dishes of their peasant forebears. Pea and lentil soups; potatoes, cabbage, and sauerkraut cooked in a hundred different ways; smoked and marinated meats; seasoned meatballs—these dishes were simply too good to be dismissed, no matter what their origin, and they became the basis of the national cuisine. In Thomas Mann's famous novel of the life of the rich German bourgeoisie, *Buddenbrooks,* there is a scene where the Buddenbrooks family hosts an elegant formal dinner. The meal, "good heavy food from good heavy silver plate," is an elaborate affair proceeding through innumerable courses. After the soup and fish have been consumed, "the plates were changed again. An enormous brick-red boiled ham appeared, strewn with crumbs and served with a sour brown onion sauce, and so many vegetables that the company could have satisfied their appetites from that one vegetable dish." Hearty food in abundance was an obvious sign of prosperity and "one could be sure of a good square meal at the Buddenbrooks'."

Germans have always taken great pleasure in eating, and it is difficult to say whether this is because their food is so good or whether their fare is excellent because of the national interest in dining. In years past, Germans ate five meals a day. Although eating patterns have changed, keeping pace with the industrialization of the country, the traditional five meals encompass the foods loved by young and old alike. First, of course, is breakfast, made up of dark breads and of fresh rolls, either home-baked or bought from the baker early in the morning. Occasionally, eggs or cheese are also served. Only a few hours later comes a second breakfast, which is a snack or a sandwich made of cheese or meat. Children carry second-breakfast bags to school; workers bring theirs to offices or factories for a more substantial coffee break than is common in the United States. In Germany, lunch is always a hot meal. A few hours after second breakfast, therefore, a German sits down to lunch, which customarily was his dinner, the big meal of the day, and progressed from soup through a fish course, then meat and vegetables, ending with a dessert—fruit, or a sweet concoction. Today the main meal is usually taken in the evening, instead, but lunch is always a hot repast. When the office and schoolroom are close enough to home, all the members of the family eat together at midday. A working housewife (and many German mothers work) prepares the family's lunch the night before and generally makes a substantial one-dish casserole. Many German firms provide employee cafeterias for those who work far from home.

The fourth meal comes between midday and evening. Similar to English tea, it is called *Kaffee,* or "coffee." For some, this meal may be a simple coffee break, but usually it is a more formal affair. Coffee alone is considered insufficient, so it is accompanied by baked delights— apple or honey cakes, tortes, cookies, or doughnuts. German cakes and pastries are rarely offered as dessert at the end of a dinner but are instead reserved for *Kaffee,* the time when the sweets themselves constitute the meal.

Dinner or supper is the fifth meal of the day. If a simple one-dish casserole makes up the midday meal, the large meal of several courses is served at the end of the workday. If midday dinner is substantial, the evening supper frequently consists of soup or a platter of cold cuts and cheeses.

As far as favorite foods are concerned, pork has been mentioned as the most frequently eaten meat in Germany. Every bit of the pig, from trotters to ears, is utilized in some fashion. Fresh, pickled, or smoked, pork forms the basis of hundreds of specialties. Sometimes it is marinated, to give the meat a taste that is probably similar to that of the wild boar. Beef, too, is frequently marinated. At one time, this was essential, for German beef was tough and had to be soaked in strong vinegar to tenderize it. Today, of course, the quality of German beef is top grade, but marinating produces such delicious results that it remains a cooking technique widely used in German kitchens, where wine, vinegar, or a mixture of both may be used.   This is the mode of preparation for one of the country's most celebrated dishes, sauerbraten.

Potatoes, cabbage, and sauerkraut are the usual accompaniments for meat.   Germany is now known as a nation of potato-eaters, but the Germans were in fact among the last Europeans to incorporate the vegetable into their diet.   The renowned King Frederick the Great, in an effort to avoid a famine, tried to persuade the German peasants to grow and eat potatoes.   The peasants, however, feared the new vegetable, believing it to be poisonous, and many superstitions sprang up about the food.   It was said, for example, that if a pregnant woman ate a potato, her child would be born lumpy and have many eyes.   Eventually the king convinced the peasants to try the new food by dispatching troops to the provinces with seed potatoes and instructions for planting. This forcible persuasion succeeded: The potatoes were planted, flourished, and slowly grew to be accepted as a mainstay of German cooking. Today, potatoes are an important part of the national diet.   They appear at most midday and evening meals and are occasionally served as a separate course in the form of pancakes, dumplings, or salads.

Cabbage also appears frequently on the German table, most often in its fermented form, sauerkraut.   The word *kraut* means "cabbage," but sometimes also refers to soured cabbage.   Although it is popularly associated with Germany, sauerkraut is not a native dish.   It is believed that the Chinese invented it, and that the Mongols learned the technique from them, carrying it across Asia and into Hungary; from Hungary it traveled to Austria and finally to Germany.   The Germans accepted sauerkraut as a delicious addition to their diet.   They varied its preparation with interesting innovations, such as adding juniper berries or caraway seeds, and made it a national dish.

The Germans have always excelled in the art of baking.   Bread, in particular, has been a mainstay of the German diet since early pagan times, when it played a part in religious rites.   It was so essential and so revered that there were many superstitions surrounding it.   Several folk tales describe what could happen to someone who did not treat the food with respect.   One story recounts the misfortunes of a girl who trod on a loaf of bread, using it as a stepping stone to help her over a muddy street.   Turned into a repulsive insect, she must remain in this state until she has properly atoned for misusing the loaf.

Some of the shapes in which Germans bake bread have religious meaning, dating from heathen days.   Historians believe that bread was offered to the gods, since it was one of the basic foods and, of course, a small loaf could be more easily spared by the peasant than one of his livestock. Its use in these pagan ceremonies led the peasants to bake loaves in special shapes—round flat loaves to represent the sun, or crescent loaves or rolls for the moon, both so important to the farmer. The braided loaves, still popular today, may originally have substituted for an offering of shorn hair. Nowadays such religious meaning has been lost, and bread and cookies are shaped or stamped with designs for reasons of tradition or for their decorative value, but the Germans still take their baking very seriously.

Many of their cakes and cookies are molded into shapes that only an artist could originally have devised. Baking in this fashion demonstrates the continuation of a three-hundred-year-old tradition. From honey-sweetened or ginger-spiced dough, German bakers in the seventeenth and eighteenth centuries created angels, babes in swaddling clothes, and lovers entwined in one another's arms, and shaped figures representing entire biblical scenes. The molds in which the cakes were baked were crafted by talented sculptors from wood, ceramic, or metal, and many of the originals can be seen today in museums. The intricately molded cakes were highly prized. They were presented as gifts and were passed around to be displayed and admired before being consumed. Sometimes the giver's portrait was engraved on a cookie. On a less elaborate scale, this artistic baking tradition is reflected in the popularity of the springerle cookie molds and rolling pins, which imprint many fanciful shapes on the cookie dough. No German housewife would be without her special rolling pin or mold. The tradition is also very much alive in the time-honored preparation of marzipan, the almond and sugar paste that is tinted with food coloring and modeled into a variety of shapes—tiny fruits, flowers, animals, and human forms.

Because they love sweets, the Germans are fond of a particular kind of restaurant—the *Konditorei*, or pastry shop, which, unfortunately, does not exist in the United States. Afternoon *Kaffee*, if it is not taken at home, is bought at the *Konditorei*, where coffee and cake are the specialties. No matter how tiny the shop may be, its assortment of sweets is lavish and attractively displayed. A pastry shop in Cologne, for example, which has only twelve tables, offers fifty-seven different cakes and pastries on its daily menu. Although German housewives frequently buy sweets at the *Konditorei* for their family's late-afternoon *Kaffee*, they are equally proud of their own efforts and they enjoy making home-baked goodies, rich with cream or laden with fruit.

With their meals the Germans consume two of the world's finest beverages—German beer and German white wine. Our beer is similar to theirs, but Germany produces many more varieties than does the United States.   In West Germany alone there are four thousand breweries, with products ranging from golden lagers to dark-brown bock beers.   Some beers are served with lemon, some with raspberry syrup.   Some contain 28 percent alcohol and some as little as 2 percent.   In Bavaria, the center of Germany's beer production, the annual per capita beer consumption is estimated at two hundred quarts.   Beer-drinking is celebrated in jovial company at outdoor beer gardens and in dark-raftered beer cellars, where neighbors lock arms, laugh, sing, gossip, and occasionally dance on the tables.

There is a special form to drinking German beer the German way. The temperature of the beer, the size and shape of the glass or stein, and the pouring of the beer itself must all be considered.   Germans like their beer a bit warmer than Americans generally do, although not quite as warm as the British prefer it.   German beer is served at about 45° Fahrenheit.   The glass must be dry and at room temperature; it may be of any shape so long as it is widest at the bottom and narrows toward the top so that the beer can hold its head.   (The Pilsner shape, seen in many American beer advertisements and used in many of our restaurants and bars, will simply not do.)   The beer's head is very important to a German beer drinker.   Too much head interferes with the consumption of the drink; too little dulls and flattens the flavor.   In Germany one always begins by pouring the beer against the side of the glass.   When it is half full, the glass is straightened, the bottle raised high, and the beer poured right into the center.   This technique produces a head about one inch high—the prescribed amount for a good drink in the German style.

The white wines of Germany are superb.   Those from the vineyards along the Rhine and Moselle rivers compare favorably with excellent French white wines; indeed, Moselle is considered by many connoisseurs to be the world's finest white wine.   It is of a delicately pale color, and its taste is remarkably light and dry.   Wines are served at a restaurant known as a *Weinstube* or wine restaurant (as opposed to a *Bierstube*, where beer is served).   Here, in an atmosphere of dignified quiet, stewards serve the wine with impeccable formality.   However, in the summer and early fall, wine lovers grow as exuberant as beer drinkers.   Throughout August and September there is a series of wine festivals in southern Germany to celebrate the grape harvest.   These occasions feature singing and dancing and great conviviality.

Germany's two drinks, her wine and her beer, reflect the two disparate images of the country—one of a formal nation, which venerates tradition and order, and the other of a joyous, fun-loving people, fond of music, dancing, and relaxation. To entertain in the German fashion, you may choose either style: an elegant German dinner party or a light-hearted supper made merrier with music and singing.

If you choose the former, the table must be set with your finest linen and dishes and it must be decorated with flowers. *Schön decken,* to set an attractive table, is an accomplishment cultivated by German homemakers. It is the skill by which they judge one another's talent for entertaining. Flowers are essential at any dinner party; in Germany, they are usually provided by the guests. It is the German practice for the guest to send the flowers *before* he arrives for dinner, so that the hostess always has the opportunity to create an artistic and imaginative table setting. This is a sensible custom that we would do well to emulate, for it is usually difficult for a hostess to do justice to gifts of flowers while welcoming her guests at the same time.

At your formal dinner party, you should serve German wine, rather than beer. The menu should begin with soup, perhaps Hearty Cabbage Soup or Split-Pea Soup with Ham. This should be followed by a meat or poultry course. Excellent choices are Tongue with Sweet-and-Sour Sauce, Sauerbraten, or Smoked Loin of Pork. With the main dish, be sure to serve some typical German accompaniments, such as Red Cabbage, Sauerkraut with Apples, or Potato Pancakes. For dessert, follow the German custom and, instead of baked goods, prepare a dish such as Macaroon Bavarian Cream with Brandied Apricots, Sour-Cream Pancakes, or Chilled Raspberry Pudding. Save the cake and cookies for later, toward midnight, just before the party is over. Late-evening coffee and cakes might include Golden Apple Strudel, Streusel-Layered Coffeecake, or Linzer Torte, which will undoubtedly be devoured right down to the last buttery crumb.

If you prefer to entertain informally—a buffet supper for a large group of friends, for example—you might have a selection of cold cuts; serve them with some of the delicious German salads and vegetables made from the recipes in this book. A hot casserole dish would be an excellent addition to your buffet table; you might prepare Knackwurst in Beer, or Sausage, Apple, and Cabbage Casserole, keeping it hot in a chafing dish. Finally, the table should be well stocked with bottles of cold beer and baskets of thick dark bread.

Either German party will create a feeling of *Gemütlichkeit,* which is best translated as an atmosphere of friendly, all-pervasive warmth. And there is nothing like a hearty German meal, shared with friends, to help capture this good feeling of camaraderie.

Appetizers & Soups

The first course at a German dinner is called *Vorspeisen,* which literally means "before foods." It is composed of such appetite-tempting delicacies as cheese mixed with onions or beer, marinated sausages, or sausage wrapped in puff pastry. Germans usually buy *Vorspeisen* rather than prepare them at home, and German appetizer establishments have an extraordinarily wide range of choices. A housewife serving the *Vorspeisen* will often set them out as one does hors d'oeuvres, for her family to make their own choices. Two German appetizers that you can make yourself are Herring in Dill Sauce and Mushrooms in White Wine. Or you can purchase an assortment of smoked fish, sausages, or spiced cold meat from the delicatessen.

Next on the menu comes soup, for in Germany a meal would be incomplete without a hearty soup. If the soup is really good, appetites may be satisfied with simply a second helping of it and no other course is necessary. German soups are thick and filled with pieces of meat, such as Yellow-Pea Soup with Pork or Lentil Soup with Ham. Others are thin broths, enriched with accompaniments such as plump tender dumplings or noodles, bread cubes, or pancakes, for example, Kraftbrühe mit Frittaten.

APPETIZERS

Cheddar-Beer Spread

½ pound mild Cheddar cheese, grated
½ clove garlic, crushed
Dash cayenne

1 tablespoon Worcestershire sauce
½ teaspoon dry mustard
½ cup beer

1. Combine cheese, garlic, cayenne, Worcestershire, mustard, and beer in medium-size bowl.

2. Mix until very smooth.

3. To store: Fill crock, and seal top with melted paraffin. Keep refrigerated several weeks. Then serve as a cocktail spread. Remove from refrigerator ½ hour before serving.

Makes 1½ cups.

Herring in Dill Sauce

1 cup prepared mustard
1 cup olive oil
¼ cup vinegar
3 tablespoons lemon juice
½ cup chopped fresh dill
1 teaspoon pepper

1½ teaspoons salt
1½ teaspoons whole allspice
2 tablespoons sugar
8 salt herring fillets

Fresh dill sprigs

1. Combine mustard and oil in small bowl; beat, with rotary beater, until as thick as mayonnaise. Gradually beat in vinegar and lemon juice, then dill, pepper, salt, allspice, and sugar.

2. Rinse herring; drain well on paper towels. Place in large glass bowl; cover with sauce. Refrigerate, covered, at least 3 days.

3. Garnish with dill sprigs, and serve as first course or as an hors d'oeuvre.

Makes about 8 servings.

Mushrooms in White Wine

1 tablespoon salt
1 pound fresh button mushrooms
½ cup chopped onion
1 clove garlic, finely chopped
¼ cup chopped parsley
2 bay leaves

⅛ teaspoon pepper
½ teaspoon dried thyme leaves
2 cups white wine
2 cups white vinegar
½ cup olive or salad oil
2 tablespoons lemon juice

1. Add salt to 6 cups cold water. Wash mushrooms in this; drain.

2. Combine remaining ingredients in large saucepan. Add mushrooms; bring to boiling point.

3. Reduce heat, and simmer, covered, 8 to 10 minutes, or until mushrooms are tender. Cool.

4. Refrigerate, covered, at least 1 hour, or until ready to use. Makes 6 servings.

Mustard Spareribs

2 pounds spareribs	2 teaspoons dry mustard
½ cup lemon juice, fresh, frozen, or canned	2 teaspoons sugar
¼ teaspoon pepper	½ cup prepared mustard

1. Have butcher crack spareribs across middle. At home, with kitchen shears, cut spareribs into finger-length pieces.

2. In a flat pan, mix ½ cup water, lemon juice, pepper, dry mustard, and sugar. Marinate spareribs in this mixture at least 2 hours (turn once during marinating).

3. Remove rack, and preheat broiler at broil or 550°F.

4. Drain spareribs; arrange on cold broiler rack. Using spatula, spread ribs with prepared mustard.

5. Place rack 4 to 5 inches from heat. Broil 10 minutes; turn ribs, and broil 5 minutes. Serve hot.
Makes hors d'oeuvres for 8.

Pâté Mold

½ pound sweet butter	1 teaspoon salt
2 large onions, sliced	Dash pepper
2½ pounds chicken livers	
3 hard-cooked eggs	Pimiento strips
¼ cup cognac	Green-pepper strips

1. In ¼ cup hot butter in skillet, sauté onions until tender—about 10 minutes. Remove from skillet.

2. Heat half of remaining butter in same skillet. Add half of chicken livers; sauté over high heat 3 to 5 minutes; remove. Repeat with the remaining butter and remaining chicken livers.

3. Place one-third onions, one-third chicken livers, 1 egg, cut up, and one-third cognac in blender; blend at low speed ½ minute, then at high speed until smooth. Turn into bowl. Repeat twice. Stir in salt and

pepper.   Turn into 1½-quart plain mold brushed lightly with salad oil; cover.   Refrigerate overnight.

4. To serve: Remove from refrigerator, and unmold.   Place on serving plate; decorate with pimiento and green-pepper strips.

Makes 6 cups, or 25 servings.

Pickled Shrimp

1 pound cleaned, cooked medium-size shrimp	1 onion, sliced
	2 teaspoons salt
1 cup vinegar	1 teaspoon sugar
3 whole cloves	
¼ teaspoon pepper	Stuffed olives
1 bay leaf	

1. Place shrimp in mixing bowl.

2. In saucepan, combine remaining ingredients; bring to a boil.   Pour mixture over shrimp, and cool.

3. Refrigerate, covered, at least 12 hours.

4. To serve: Drain shrimp, and spear each on a wooden pick with a stuffed olive.   Broil, and serve hot.

Makes 26 to 30, or about 6 servings.

Sweet-and-Sour Sausages

1 pound cocktail-size frankfurters	2 tablespoons light-brown sugar
1 can (8 ounces) tomato sauce	1 teaspoon Worcestershire sauce
¼ cup pineapple juice	½ lime or lemon, sliced (optional)
3 tablespoons cider vinegar	

1. With two-tined fork, pierce each frankfurter twice, all the way through.

2. In medium-size saucepan, bring 1 quart water to boiling. Add frankfurters; bring just to boiling.   Remove from heat; let stand, covered, 8 minutes.

3. Meanwhile, in medium-size saucepan, combine tomato sauce, pineapple juice, vinegar, brown sugar, and Worcestershire; heat just to boiling.

4. Drain frankfurters; add to sauce.   Baste well; then simmer, covered, 10 minutes.

5. Remove from heat; stir in lime slices.   Turn into chafing dish to serve.

Makes 28 to 36, or about 10 servings.

SOUPS

Kraftbrühe mit Frittaten

Frittaten
1 cup milk
1 egg
1 cup unsifted all-purpose flour
¼ teaspoon salt
2 tablespoons chopped parsley

Salad oil

4 cans (10½-ounce size) condensed beef consommé, undiluted

Chopped parsley

1. Make Frittaten: In medium-size bowl, with rotary beater, beat milk and egg until well mixed. Add flour and salt; beat until very smooth. Stir in 2 tablespoons parsley.

2. Slowly heat 7-inch skillet until a drop of water sizzles and rolls off. Brush lightly with oil. Pour in about 1½ tablespoons batter, rotating pan quickly to spread batter completely over bottom of pan.

3. Cook over medium heat until lightly browned on each side. Remove, and roll up loosely. Set aside. Repeat until all batter is used. Then slice each roll crosswise very thinly, to make fine pancake strips.

4. In medium-size saucepan, heat consommé with 2 cans water.

5. To serve: Heap pancake strips in soup bowls. Pour in consommé, and garnish with chopped parsley.

Makes 8 to 10 servings.

Hearty Cabbage Soup

½ pound frankfurters or knackwurst
¼ cup finely chopped onion
½ cup diced celery
1 cup diced pared raw potato
1 can (13¾ ounces) clear chicken broth
3 cups milk

2 cups finely chopped cabbage
2 teaspoons salt
¼ teaspoon pepper
2 teaspoons brown sugar
1 teaspoon caraway seed, tied in cheesecloth bag
1 cup light cream

1. Cut frankfurters into ¼-inch slices or knackwurst into chunks.

2. In 4-quart kettle, combine frankfurters, onion, celery, potato, and chicken broth; bring to boiling. Reduce heat; simmer, covered, 15 minutes.

3. Add milk, cabbage, salt, pepper, brown sugar, and caraway seed; bring back to boiling. Reduce heat; simmer, covered, 25 minutes longer.

4. Discard caraway seed.   Stir in light cream.   Serve hot.
Makes about 2 quarts; 6 to 8 servings.

Lentil Soup

½ pound (1½ cups) lentils	3 tablespoons butter or
4 slices raw bacon	margarine
1 cup chopped leek	3 tablespoons flour
½ cup chopped onion	1 can (10½ ounces) con-
¼ cup chopped carrot	densed beef broth, undiluted
¾ cup chopped green pepper	2 teaspoons salt
¾ cup chopped tomato	2 tablespoons vinegar

1. Put lentils in 5 cups cold water in large kettle; bring to boil.   Reduce heat; simmer, covered, 1 hour.

2. Meanwhile, cut bacon in small pieces; sauté, in large skillet, until crisp.   Add leek, onion, carrot, pepper, and tomato; sauté over low heat about 5 minutes.   Combine with lentils in kettle.

3. Melt butter in same skillet; remove from heat.   Stir in flour until smooth; then gradually stir in beef broth.

4. Add salt and vinegar; bring to boiling point, stirring.   Pour into lentils; cook over low heat, stirring occasionally, about 30 minutes.
Makes 6 servings.

Lentil Soup with Ham

2 pounds fully cooked ham shank	1¾ teaspoons salt
	¼ teaspoon dried thyme leaves
1½ cups dried lentils	¼ teaspoon coarsely ground
3 tablespoons butter or	black pepper
margarine	1 cup sliced frankfurters
½ cup chopped celery	(about 3)
½ cup chopped leek	
½ cup chopped onion	Dairy sour cream
1 small clove garlic, crushed	Chopped parsley

1. Trim excess fat from ham shank.

2. In large kettle, combine ham shank and lentils with 5 cups cold water; bring to boiling.

3. Reduce heat; simmer, covered, 1 hour.

4. Meanwhile, melt butter in medium-size skillet.   Add celery, leek, onion, and garlic; sauté 5 minutes.

5. Add sautéed vegetables, salt, thyme, pepper, and 2 cups water to ham shank and lentils.   Simmer, covered, until lentils are tender—about 30 minutes.

6. Remove ham from soup; cool. Then cut meat from bone, and dice.

7. With potato masher, mash vegetables right in kettle; leave some lentils whole.

8. Add diced ham to soup, along with frankfurters; simmer, covered, 30 minutes longer. (For a very thick soup, simmer uncovered.)

9. Serve topped with sour cream and parsley.

Makes 8 cups, or 8 servings.

Easy Green-Pea Soup

3 cans (10½-ounce size) condensed green-pea soup, undiluted
3 knackwurst (about 1 pound), washed
1½ cups finely chopped celery
1 cup finely chopped onion
½ cup chopped leeks
2 tablespoons chopped parsley
⅛ teaspoon dried rosemary leaves
1 bay leaf

1. In a 4-quart kettle, combine soup with 4 cups water.

2. Bring to boiling over medium heat, stirring constantly.

3. Slash knackwurst at 1-inch intervals about one-quarter through. Add to soup with celery, onion, leeks, 1 tablespoon parsley, the rosemary, and bay leaf.

4. Simmer, covered, over low heat about 20 minutes, or until knackwurst is tender.

5. Turn into soup tureen. Sprinkle with remaining parsley.

Makes about 2 quarts, or 8 servings.

Split-Pea Soup with Ham

1 (2½-pound size) ready-to-eat ham shank
1½ cups quick-cooking split green peas
1 medium-size carrot, pared and cut in 1-inch pieces
1 medium-size potato, pared and sliced
1 medium-size onion, sliced
1½ teaspoons salt
Dash pepper

Sliced pumpernickel (optional)
Sweet butter (optional)

1. Trim excess fat from ham shank.

2. In 8-quart kettle, combine ham shank with peas, carrot, potato, onion, salt, pepper, and 6 cups water; bring to boiling.

3. Reduce heat; simmer, covered, 1 hour, or until peas and ham are fork-tender.

4. Remove ham from soup; cool.   Then cut ham from bone, and dice.

5. With potato masher, mash vegetables right in kettle, until soup is smooth.

6. Add diced ham to soup.   Add more salt, if desired.   Simmer, covered, 15 minutes.   For a very thick soup, heat it uncovered.   If desired, serve with slices of pumpernickel and sweet butter.

Makes 7 cups, or 6 to 8 servings.

Split-Pea Soup with Knackwurst

1   pound quick-cooking dried
    split green peas (2¼ cups)
⅛ pound salt pork or bacon,
    coarsely chopped (⅓ cup)
1½ cups coarsely chopped
    celery
1   cup coarsely chopped onion
½ cup coarsely chopped leeks
    (optional)
2   or 3 pig's knuckles (¾
    pound each)

2   parsley sprigs
1½ teaspoons salt
⅛ teaspoon dried rosemary
    leaves
1   bay leaf
3   knackwurst (about 1 pound),
    washed

Chopped parsley

1. In a deep, 8-quart kettle, combine peas and 2 quarts water; bring to boiling.   Reduce heat, and simmer, covered, 45 minutes.

2. Meanwhile, in skillet, sauté pork several minutes.   Add celery, onion, leeks; sauté until onion is golden, about 5 minutes.

3. Wipe pig's knuckles with damp paper towels.   Add to peas with sautéed salt-pork mixture, the parsley sprigs, salt, rosemary, and bay leaf; bring to boiling.   Reduce heat, and simmer, covered, 2 hours, or until pig's knuckles are tender.   Remove from heat.

4. Remove pig's knuckles with slotted spoon.   Remove their skin and excess fat.   If desired, take meat off bones.

5. If necessary, skim fat from soup.   Put soup, with vegetables, through coarse sieve, puréeing vegetables.   Pour back into kettle.

6. Slash knackwurst at 1-inch intervals about one quarter through. Add to soup with pig's knuckles or meat and a little water if soup is too thick.   Simmer, covered, 30 to 40 minutes.   Turn into soup tureen, and garnish with chopped parsley.

7. When serving, lift knackwurst out of soup.   Cut into slices.   Serve separately or in servings of soup.

Makes about 2½ quarts, or 8 servings.

Note: Flavor is improved if soup is made one day, refrigerated, then reheated and served next day.

Yellow-Pea Soup with Pork

1 pound quick-cooking dried
   split yellow peas (2¼ cups)
1 bay leaf
1 (2½-pound size) pork
   shoulder, bone in
1 cup finely chopped onion
3 teaspoons salt

1 teaspoon dried marjoram
   leaves
½ teaspoon ground ginger
¼ teaspoon dried thyme leaves
¼ teaspoon pepper

Lemon slices

1. In deep, 8-quart kettle, combine peas, bay leaf, and 2 quarts water; bring to boiling. Reduce heat, and simmer 1 hour, covered, stirring occasionally.

2. Add pork shoulder, onion, salt, marjoram, ginger, thyme, and pepper; bring to boiling. Reduce heat and simmer, covered, stirring occasionally, 2 hours, or until pork is tender. (If soup seems too thick, stir in a little water—about ½ cup.)

3. Turn into soup tureen, and garnish with lemon slices.

4. When serving, lift pork out of soup. Cut into slices. Serve with mustard, if desired.

Makes about 2 quarts, or 6 to 8 servings.

Note: Flavor is improved if soup is made one day, refrigerated, then reheated and served next day.

Vegetables

The German repertoire of vegetable cookery is not quite so extensive as the American, but the vegetables that are favored are temptingly prepared. The German climate is not conducive to growing the less hearty greens, and in parts of the country the only vegetables that survive the cold are those that can be stored in cellars during the winter season—beets, turnips, carrots, members of the cabbage family, and the ubiquitous potato.

The potato appears in so many different guises in German cooking that sometimes it is hard to recognize the vegetable. It may be molded into dumplings (see page 23). It may be fried into pancakes (see page 23). Or it may be combined with other vegetables to produce a delicious hot or cold potato salad (see pp. 24–25).

A salad in Germany is usually made of cooked rather than raw vegetables. It is served either hot or cold in a tart vinegar-and-oil dressing. Customarily the salad is placed on the same plate as the meat and hot vegetables.

Seasonal vegetables, available for only a short period of time, are highly regarded. Some, such as fresh white asparagus, are reserved for special occasions or for company dinners, when they are served as a separate course. German mushrooms are another vegetable to receive special treatment. Many delicious varieties are carefully cultivated, and mushrooms cooked with celery (see page 22) provide an elegant vegetable side dish.

Red Cabbage

1 medium-size head red cabbage	½ cup cider vinegar
2 tablespoons salt	½ cup sugar
2 tablespoons butter or margarine	2 tart red cooking apples
	1 tablespoon flour

1. Remove outer leaves from cabbage, and discard. Cut cabbage into quarters; cut out core. Shred cabbage. Measure 10 cups.

2. In large skillet, combine cabbage, salt, butter, vinegar, sugar, and ½ cup cold water.

3. Cook, covered, over medium heat, stirring occasionally, 15 minutes.

4. Meanwhile, core the apples, but do not pare. Slice thinly. Add to cabbage; cook 10 minutes longer, or until the cabbage is tender but still crisp.

5. Sprinkle flour over cabbage mixture; mix gently. Cook, stirring, until mixture thickens.

Makes 6 servings.

Sautéed Celery with Mushrooms

1 bunch celery	⅛ teaspoon pepper
2 tablespoons butter or margarine	⅛ teaspoon paprika
1 teaspoon salt	1 can (4 ounces) sliced mushrooms, drained

1. Clean celery, and cut stalks diagonally in ¼-inch slices—there will be about 6 cups.

2. Heat butter in large skillet. Add celery. Sprinkle with salt, pepper, and paprika; cook over high heat, stirring, about 8 minutes, or until tender.

3. Add mushrooms; cook 2 minutes longer.

Makes 6 servings.

Caraway Noodles

1 tablespoon salt	¼ cup melted butter or margarine
1 package (8 ounces) medium-size noodles	1 tablespoon caraway seed

1. In large kettle, bring 3 quarts water and the salt to a rapid boil. Add noodles.

2. Bring back to boiling; cook, uncovered, stirring occasionally, 7 to 10 minutes, or just until noodles are tender.

3. Turn into colander; drain.   Return noodles to kettle.   Add butter and caraway seed; toss lightly to combine.

Makes 6 servings.

Fried Potatoes

4 medium-size potatoes (about 1¼ pounds), pared	¼ cup butter or margarine Salt and pepper

1. Slice potatoes, crosswise, into ⅛-inch-thick slices.

2. In hot butter in large skillet, sauté potato slices, turning occasionally, until golden brown and tender.

3. Sprinkle with salt and pepper.

Makes 4 servings.

Potato Dumplings

3 pounds medium-size potatoes	½ cup packaged dry bread crumbs
Salt	
Dash pepper	¼ cup chopped parsley
2 eggs	¼ teaspoon nutmeg
1 cup unsifted all-purpose flour	

1. Cook unpared potatoes in boiling water, covered, until tender— about ½ hour.   Drain; cool slightly; peel.

2. Put potatoes through ricer; spread on paper towels to dry well. Place in large bowl; toss with 2½ teaspoons salt and the pepper.   Make a well in center; break eggs into well.   Sift ¾ cup flour over eggs.   Add bread crumbs, parsley, and nutmeg.   With hands, work mixture until it is smooth and holds together.

3. Shape into 16 egg-shaped dumplings.   Roll in remaining flour.

4. In large saucepan, bring about 2 quarts lightly salted water to boiling point; reduce heat.

5. Drop in just enough dumplings to fit comfortably in pan.   Boil gently, uncovered, 2 minutes after they rise to surface.   (Break one open to test for doneness.   Cook others longer, if necessary.)   Drain on paper towels.   Serve hot with Sauerbraten, if desired (see p. 30).

Makes 8 servings.

Potato Pancakes

4 large potatoes (2 pounds), pared	Dash nutmeg Dash pepper
¼ cup grated onion	Salad oil or shortening for frying
2 eggs, slightly beaten	
2 tablespoons flour	Chilled applesauce or dairy sour cream
¾ teaspoon salt	

1. On medium grater, grate potatoes. Drain very well; pat dry with dish towel; measure 3 cups.

2. In large bowl, combine grated potato with onion, eggs, flour, salt, nutmeg, and pepper.

3. In large, heavy skillet, slowly heat oil, ⅛ inch deep, until very hot but not smoking.

4. For each pancake, drop 2 tablespoons potato mixture at a time into hot fat. With spatula, flatten against bottom of skillet to make a pancake 4 inches in diameter. Fry 2 or 3 minutes on each side, or until golden brown.

5. Drain well on paper towels. Serve hot with applesauce or sour cream.

Makes 12, or about 5 servings.

Potato Salad

3 pounds medium-size potatoes	1 teaspoon salt
1 cup bottled Italian-style dressing	¼ teaspoon dill seed
1 cup diced celery	1 cup mayonnaise or cooked salad dressing
½ cup finely chopped green pepper	2 tablespoons prepared mustard
¼ cup diced pimiento	
2 tablespoons chopped onion	Salad greens

1. In boiling, salted water to cover, cook unpared potatoes, covered, just until tender—30 to 35 minutes.

2. Drain; cool 10 minutes. Peel, and slice into a large bowl. Pour Italian-style dressing over potato slices; toss lightly.

3. In medium-size bowl, combine remaining ingredients (except salad greens); mix well. Add to potato; toss lightly to combine.

4. Refrigerate, covered, until well chilled—3 or more hours.

5. To serve, spoon into serving bowl. Garnish with salad greens.
Makes about 8 servings.

Hot Potato Salad

3 pounds medium-size potatoes	2 tablespoons chopped parsley
1½ teaspoons salt	9 slices raw bacon, finely cut up
⅛ teaspoon pepper	1 tablespoon flour
⅔ cup chopped onion	½ cup white vinegar
½ cup sliced radishes	2 tablespoons sugar
½ teaspoon celery seed	

1. Cook unpeeled potatoes, covered, in boiling water just until tender—about 30 minutes.   *Do not overcook.*

2. Drain potatoes; cool, peel, and cut into cubes.   Put in serving bowl.

3. Toss lightly—be careful not to break potato cubes—with salt, pepper, onion, radishes, celery seed, and parsley.

4. Sauté bacon in skillet, over low heat, until crisp; remove from heat. With slotted spoon, remove bacon; add to potatoes.

5. Drain from skillet all but 1 tablespoon bacon fat.   Stir in flour until smooth.   Gradually add vinegar and ½ cup water.   Stir in sugar; bring to boiling point, stirring.

6. Toss lightly with potato mixture until thoroughly combined.   Serve warm.

Makes 6 servings.

Hot Potato Salad with Sausage

¾ pound kielbasa	¼ cup finely chopped onion
1 small onion, sliced	1 tablespoon flour
2 pounds potatoes, pared and sliced	1 teaspoon sugar
½ teaspoon salt	⅓ cup cider vinegar
6 slices raw bacon	¼ cup dried pimiento

1. In medium-size saucepan, cover sausage with cold water.   Add sliced onion; bring to boiling. Reduce heat; simmer, covered, 30 minutes.

2. Remove sausage from cooking liquid.   Drain cooking liquid, reserving ⅓ cup.   Cut sausage into chunks.

3. Cook potatoes, with the salt, in 1 inch boiling water, covered, 15 to 20 minutes, or just until potatoes are tender.   Drain.

4. Meanwhile, in small skillet, sauté bacon until crisp.   Remove bacon from skillet; drain well on paper towels.   Crumble, and set aside.

5. Pour off all but ⅓ cup drippings from skillet.   In drippings, sauté chopped onion 5 minutes.

6. Combine flour and sugar.   Stir into mixture in skillet.   Add vinegar and reserved cooking liquid from sausage; bring to boiling, stirring. Remove from heat.

7. In large bowl, gently combine sausage, hot potatoes, bacon, pimiento, vinegar dressing.   Serve at once.

Makes 6 servings.

Sauerkraut with Apples

2 tablespoons butter or margarine

3 tablespoons chopped onion

2 cans (1-pound size) sauerkraut (1 quart), drained

2 cups pared, sliced tart cooking apples

1 can (10½ ounces) condensed beef broth, undiluted

2 tablespoons cider vinegar

1 tablespoon flour

½ cup grated raw potato

⅛ teaspoon caraway seed

1. In hot butter in large skillet, sauté onion until golden—about 3 minutes. Add sauerkraut, apples, beef broth, and vinegar; simmer, uncovered, 15 minutes.

2. Mix flour with 2 tablespoons water until smooth.

3. Stir into sauerkraut, along with potato and caraway seed; cook over medium heat, stirring, 5 minutes, or until slightly thickened.

Makes 6 servings.

Meat & Poultry

Germans like to pot-roast meat. Although they also cook their roasts in an oven, they more often prefer to stew or pot the meat with vegetables in a hearty stock. In former times, when German beef was tougher and had to marinate or cook slowly in a sauce to become tender and flavorful, potting or stewing was a necessity. Today the wonderful taste of marinated pot roasts is reason enough to continue the old tradition.

The favorite beef dish in Germany is Sauerbraten—marinated beef flavored with spices such as cloves, ginger, or allspice, then slowly pot-roasted. Accompanied by red cabbage and potato dumplings, it is Germany's national dish, having the same eminence as does roast beef and Yorkshire pudding in England. A favorite veal recipe is Schnitzel in Holstein Sauce. *Schnitzel* means "cutlet," and Germans prepare several kinds of veal cutlets—breaded cutlets, cutlets spread with cheese and ham, cutlets wrapped in pancakes. Schnitzel in Holstein Sauce is the most elaborate veal dish, however. It was named after a diplomat who liked many good things to be served on one plate, so the schnitzel devised in his honor is accompanied by anchovies and eggs, and sometimes by smoked salmon, mushrooms, and truffles.

Game meats, which are not readily available in the United States, are very popular in Germany. Rabbit, venison steaks, wild boar, and even bear meat from the Black Forest can be purchased at butcher shops. While Germany's forests have always sheltered a variety of game animals, at earlier times only the nobility were allowed to hunt there. Perhaps it is the memory of those days of deprivation that accounts for the pleasure Germans take in cooking game dishes. Hasenpfeffer, or stewed rabbit, is prepared in several different ways, as are venison and pheasant.

Poultry, too, is popular. Chicken, for example, is consumed in enormous quantities, and Germans are even more enthusiastic about duck and goose. Duck appears in several outstanding main dishes, such as the classic Duckling in May Wine.

MEAT

Beef Roulades

2 (1½-pound size) round steaks, ¼ inch thick	2 large dill pickles, each cut into three strips
Salt	Flour
Pepper	¼ cup salad oil
1½ teaspoons brown mustard	1 can (10½ ounces) con-
6 tablespoons chopped onion	densed beef broth, undiluted
3 slices raw bacon, halved crosswise	

1. Wipe beef with damp paper towels. Cut each steak crosswise into three equal pieces. Pound each with a mallet or edge of saucer, to flatten to ⅛-inch thickness.

2. Sprinkle lightly with salt and pepper; spread each with ¼ teaspoon mustard; then sprinkle each with 1 tablespoon chopped onion.

3. Place a bacon piece, then a pickle strip, across narrow end of each piece of steak.

4. Roll up, starting from narrow end; tie with twine. Sprinkle lightly with about 2 tablespoons flour.

5. In heavy skillet or Dutch oven with tight-fitting cover, slowly heat salad oil. In hot oil, brown roulades on all sides until nicely browned— 15 to 20 minutes. Add beef broth; bring to boiling; reduce heat, and simmer, covered, about 1½ hours, or until tender.

6. With slotted spoon, remove roulades to heated serving platter. Remove twine. Keep warm.

7. Pour drippings from skillet into a 2-cup measure. Skim fat from surface, and discard. Add water to measure 1 cup, if necessary. Return to skillet.

8. In small bowl, combine 1½ tablespoons flour with 3 tablespoons water, stirring, to form a smooth paste.

9. Stir into drippings in skillet. Bring to boiling; reduce heat, and simmer, stirring, until thickened and smooth.

10. Pour gravy over roulades.   Serve with buttered noodles and Red Cabbage if desired (see p. 22).

Makes 3 or 4 servings.

Filet of Beef with May Wine Sauce

1 pound filet of beef	**Wine Sauce**
Salt	6 shallots, chopped
Pepper	1 cup May Wine
6 tablespoons butter or	2 tablespoons chopped parsley
margarine	2 tablespoons lemon juice

1. Cut filet into slices, about ¼-inch thick.   Sprinkle lightly with salt and pepper.

2. In 4 tablespoons hot butter in large skillet over high heat, quickly brown filet slices on each side—about 1 minute per side.   Arrange on serving platter; keep warm.

3. Add remaining butter and shallots to skillet; sauté until golden brown.   Stir in wine; bring to boiling.   Add parsley and lemon.   Taste and add salt and pepper, if needed.

4. To serve, pour a little of the sauce over filet and pass the rest.

Makes 4 servings.

Stuffed Green-Cabbage Rolls

1 large head green cabbage (about 2½ pounds)	1 can (10½ ounces) condensed beef consommé, undiluted
Filling	
1 pound ground beef chuck	2 tablespoons butter or margarine
2 cups cooked white rice	2 tablespoons light-brown sugar
½ cup chopped onion	2 tablespoons flour
1 egg	1 medium-size onion, sliced
1 teaspoon salt	1 can (1 pound) whole tomatoes, undrained
1 teaspoon Worcestershire sauce	½ teaspoon salt
⅛ teaspoon pepper	

1. In large saucepan, bring 6 cups water to boiling.   Remove 12 large outer leaves from cabbage; trim thick rib of each leaf for easier rolling. (Use remaining cabbage another day.)

2. Add leaves to boiling water.   Remove from heat and let stand 2 minutes—just long enough to make leaves pliable.   Drain well.

3. Make Filling: In medium-size bowl, combine beef, rice, onion, egg,

salt, Worcestershire, pepper, and ½ cup consommé (set aside remaining consommé); mix until well blended.

4. Preheat oven to 350°F.

5. Place ⅓ cup filling in center of each cabbage leaf. Fold two sides over filling; roll up from end. Secure with wooden picks.

6. Melt butter and brown sugar in skillet. Add cabbage rolls, and sauté until glazed on all sides—about 5 minutes. Arrange in 3-quart casserole.

7. Combine flour with reserved consommé, mixing until smooth. Add to skillet with onion, tomatoes, and salt; bring to boiling, stirring; mixture will thicken slightly. Pour over cabbage rolls.

8. Bake, covered, 1 hour and 15 minutes.

Makes 6 servings.

Sauerbraten

2 ounces salt pork, cut into strips about ¼ inch wide	**Marinade**
	2 cups cider vinegar
1 medium-size onion, finely chopped	3 medium-size onions, sliced
	12 whole black peppercorns
1 tablespoon salt	6 whole cloves
1½ teaspoons pepper	1 bay leaf
1 teaspoon grated lemon peel	
½ teaspoon ground allspice	1 tablespoon sugar
1 (5-pound size) top-round or rump beef roast, rolled and tied	2 tablespoons flour
	Salt
	Pepper

1. In small bowl, combine salt-pork strips with chopped onion, 1 tablespoon salt, 1½ teaspoons pepper, the lemon peel, and allspice.

2. Wipe roast with damp paper towels. Push handle of wooden spoon through one end of roast almost to other end. Repeat twice, making 3 openings in all. Pack openings with pork mixture; place in large bowl.

3. Make Marinade: In medium-size saucepan, combine vinegar, 1 cup water, the onion, peppercorns, whole cloves, and bay leaf; bring to boiling. Pour over roast.

4. Refrigerate, covered, 3 days. Turn meat once a day.

5. Preheat oven to 350°F. Remove meat from marinade, and place in deep roasting pan or Dutch oven. Stir sugar into marinade; pour over meat. Heat on top of stove until marinade just comes to boiling.

6. Roast, covered, basting frequently, 2 hours, or until meat is very tender.

7. Remove meat to heated serving platter; remove string. Keep warm.

8. Strain pan liquid, pressing onions through strainer. Skim off fat, Liquid should measure 2½ cups. Mix flour with ¼ cup water. Stir into strained liquid; bring to boiling. Reduce heat, and simmer 3 minutes. Add salt and pepper to taste. Pour some gravy over roast; pass rest.

9. If desired, serve with Potato Dumplings (see p. 23) and hot stewed prunes.

Makes 7 or 8 servings.

Sauerbraten with Gingersnaps

Marinade
1 cup cider vinegar
1 cup Burgundy
2 onions, sliced
1 carrot, sliced
1 stalk celery, chopped
2 whole allspice
4 whole cloves
1 tablespoon salt

1½ teaspoons pepper

1 (4-pound-size) rump or boned chuck pot roast
4 tablespoons unsifted all-purpose flour
⅓ cup salad oil
1 tablespoon sugar
½ cup crushed gingersnaps

1. In large bowl, combine vinegar, Burgundy, onion, carrot, celery, allspice, cloves, salt, and pepper.

2. Wipe meat with damp paper towels. Put in marinade; refrigerate, covered, 3 days, turning meat occasionally.

3. Remove meat from the marinade. Reserve marinade. Wipe meat dry with paper towels. Coat with 2 tablespoons flour.

4. In hot oil in Dutch oven, over medium heat, brown meat well on all sides.

5. Pour in marinade; simmer, covered, 2½ to 3 hours, or until meat is tender.

6. Remove meat from Dutch oven. Press liquid and vegetables through coarse sieve; skim off fat. Measure 3½ cups liquid (add water, if necessary). Return liquid to Dutch oven.

7. Mix remaining 2 tablespoons flour with ⅓ cup cold water and the sugar. Stir into liquid; bring to boiling, stirring. Stir in gingersnaps.

8. Return meat to the Dutch oven. Spoon gravy over it; simmer, covered, 20 minutes.

9. Remove meat to heated platter. Pour some of gravy over it. Serve meat, thinly sliced, with more gravy. If desired, serve with Caraway Noodles (see p. 22) and Red Cabbage (see p. 22).

Makes 6 servings.

German Meatballs with Sauerkraut

Meatballs
1 egg
½ cup soft bread crumbs
1½ pounds ground chuck
1 can (14 ounces) sauerkraut, drained and chopped
1 can (1 pound, 4 ounces) apple slices, drained and chopped
2 tablespoons grated onion
Salt

Pepper
¼ teaspoon dried marjoram leaves, crumbled

4 slices raw bacon, diced
½ cup chopped onion
½ teaspoon caraway seed
1 cup canned chicken broth
1 tablespoon sugar
1 cup dairy sour cream

1. In medium-size bowl, beat egg well. Add bread crumbs, chuck, ¼ cup sauerkraut, ¾ cup chopped apple, the grated onion, 1 teaspoon salt, ½ teaspoon pepper, and the marjoram; mix with fork until well blended. Shape into 20 meatballs.

2. In 4-quart Dutch oven, sauté bacon until crisp. Remove, and set aside. In hot drippings, brown meatballs on all sides. Remove, and set aside.

3. In Dutch oven, combine remaining sauerkraut and chopped apple, the chopped onion, caraway seed, chicken broth, sugar, ¼ teaspoon salt, and ⅛ teaspoon pepper; stir until well blended. Bring to boiling, covered.

4. Arrange meatballs on top; cook over low heat, covered, until heated through. Remove from heat; stir in sour cream.

5. To serve, sprinkle with bacon bits, and, if desired, serve with boiled or mashed potatoes.

Makes 5 or 6 servings.

German Meatballs with Caper Sauce

Meatballs
2 pounds boneless veal
¼ pound pork fat
2 tablespoons butter or margarine
1 cup finely chopped onion
1 cup packaged herb-seasoned stuffing mix
1 teaspoon grated lemon peel
1 teaspoon anchovy paste
1 teaspoon salt
½ teaspoon pepper
2 teaspoons Worcestershire sauce

¼ cup chopped parsley
2 eggs, beaten

3 cans (10½-ounce size) condensed beef broth, undiluted
1 cup dry white wine

Sauce
¼ cup butter or margarine
¼ cup unsifted all-purpose flour
¼ cup drained bottled capers
½ teaspoon anchovy paste

2 tablespoons chopped parsley

1. Make Meatballs: Have butcher grind veal with pork fat.

2. In 2 tablespoons hot butter in small skillet, sauté onion until tender—about 3 minutes.

3. In large bowl, combine onion with ground veal, stuffing mix, lemon peel, 1 teaspoon anchovy paste, salt, pepper, Worcestershire, ¼ cup parsley, and eggs.   Mix well with hands to combine.

4. With moistened hands, shape mixture into meatballs, 2 inches in diameter.

5. Meanwhile, in large kettle, bring beef broth and wine to boiling. Drop meatballs, one by one, into boiling liquid.

6. Return the mixture to boiling.   Reduce heat, and simmer, covered, 20 minutes.

7. With slotted spoon, remove meatballs from cooking liquid.   Keep warm.   Strain liquid, reserving 3 cups.

8. Make Sauce: Melt ¼ cup butter in large kettle; remove from heat. Add flour, stirring to make a smooth mixture.

9. Gradually stir in reserved liquid; bring to boiling, stirring.   Add capers and ½ teaspoon anchovy paste.

10. Add meatballs to sauce; cover the kettle, and return the mixture to boiling.

11. Remove from heat.   Stir in 2 tablespoons parsley.   Serve meatballs with cooked noodles or hot, boiled potatoes, if desired.

Makes 6 to 8 servings.

Schnitzel in Holstein Sauce

8 veal scallops (about 1¼ pounds)	**Sauce**
½ cup unsifted all-purpose flour	⅓ cup butter or margarine, melted
1 egg, beaten	1 hard-cooked egg, sieved
½ cup milk	1 can (2 ounces) anchovies, drained and chopped
½ cup grated Parmesan cheese	⅛ teaspoon pepper
1 teaspoon salt	¼ cup lemon juice
½ teaspoon pepper	1½ tablespoons chopped parsley
½ teaspon nutmeg	
Salad oil or shortening for deep-frying	

1. Have butcher pound veal as for scallopini.   Or place each scallop between 2 sheets of heavy waxed paper; pound with edge of saucer to flatten.

2. Rub about ¼ cup flour into veal, turning on both sides.

3. In medium-size bowl, combine egg, milk, cheese, salt, pepper, nutmeg, and remaining flour.   Beat with rotary beater, just until smooth.

4. In electric skillet or deep-fat fryer, slowly heat oil (about ¾ inch) to 375°F. on deep-frying thermometer.

5. Dip veal, a few pieces at a time, into batter to coat evenly on both sides.

6. Fry veal, a few pieces at a time, 4 to 8 minutes, or until tender and golden brown, turning several times to brown evenly.

7. Lift veal from fat with slotted spoon; drain on paper towels. Keep warm while frying rest.

8. Make Sauce: Into butter in saucepan, stir egg, anchovies, and pepper; heat several minutes. Stir in lemon juice and parsley.

9. To serve, pour sauce over veal.

Makes 4 servings.

Veal Pot Pie

2 tablespoons salad oil	1½ tablespoons butter or
3 pounds boneless veal, cut	margarine
into 3-inch cubes	1 egg, beaten
2 teaspoons salt	
¼ teaspoon pepper	1 large onion, coarsely
3½ cups boiling water	chopped (¾ cup)
	3 cups pared, diced potatoes
Dumpling Squares	(1 pound)
1½ cups sifted all-purpose flour	3 tablespoons chopped parsley
½ teaspoon salt	1 teaspoon paprika
1 teaspoon baking powder	

1. In hot oil in 4½- to 5-quart Dutch oven, brown veal well, turning on all sides—15 to 20 minutes in all. Sprinkle with salt and pepper.

2. Add water; bring to boiling; reduce heat, and simmer, covered, 45 minutes, or until veal is almost tender.

3. Meanwhile, make Dumpling Squares: Into medium-size bowl, sift flour with salt and baking powder. With pastry blender or 2 knives, cut in butter until particles are size of large peas.

4. With fork, quickly stir in egg and 3 to 4 tablespoons cold water. (Dough will be rather stiff, but should clean side of bowl.)

5. On lightly floured surface, roll dough ⅛ inch thick, to form a rectangle that is approximately 12 by 6 inches.

6. With sharp knife, cut dough into 1½-inch squares. Let stand, uncovered, several minutes.

7. Meanwhile add onion, potatoes, 2 tablespoons parsley, and paprika to veal in Dutch oven. Simmer, covered, 10 minutes.

8. Remove cover; drop half of dumpling squares, one by one, into

simmering liquid.   As they drop to the bottom of the Dutch oven, add
the rest of the squares, stirring in carefully.

9. Simmer, covered, 25 minutes, or until dumplings are light and
cooked through.   Sprinkle top with remaining chopped parsley.

Makes 6 to 8 servings.

Sautéed Liver à la Berliner

1½ pounds beef liver, sliced ¼ inch thick	Salt
1 cup milk	⅓ cup flour
8 tablespoons butter or margarine	⅛ teaspoon pepper
4 medium-size onions, thinly sliced	2 medium-size red apples
	Parsley

1. Wash liver.   Place in shallow pan.   Add milk, turning slices to
coat well.   Refrigerate ½ hour.

2. Heat 4 tablespoons butter in large skillet.   Add onion slices and
⅛ teaspoon salt; cook over low heat, stirring occasionally, until onion
begins to brown—about 15 minutes.

3. Meanwhile, drain liver well.   Combine flour, 1 teaspoon salt, and
the pepper; use flour mixture to coat liver well.

4. Wash and core apples; trim ends, and cut each crosswise into 3
slices.   Add to skillet with onion, and cook until golden on each side
and tender—about 10 minutes.

5. Heat remaining butter in another large skillet.   Add liver slices,
and sauté until golden brown on each side—3 to 4 minutes per side.

6. To serve, place liver on heated platter.   Top with onion and apple
slices; garnish with parsley.

Makes 4 to 6 servings.

Smoked Tongue with Fruit Sauce

1 (4-pound size) smoked beef tongue	1 cup orange juice
2 cans (1-pound size) stewed tomatoes	¼ teaspoon salt
2 cans (8½-ounce size) crushed pineapple, drained	⅛ teaspoon pepper
2 tablespoons lemon juice	1 tablespoon cornstarch
	1 can (1 pound, 14 ounces) large pear halves, drained

1. In large kettle, cover tongue with cold water.

2. Bring to boiling.   Reduce heat and simmer, covered, 2 hours.

3. Drain tongue; let cool slightly.   Trim off fat and gristle at root

end. With tip of paring knife, slit skin on underside from thick end to tip. Carefully peel off; discard.

4. In same kettle, combine tomatoes, pineapple, lemon juice, orange juice, salt, and pepper; mix well. Bring to boiling. Reduce heat, and simmer, uncovered, 5 minutes.

5. Add tongue; simmer, covered, 1½ hours, or until tongue is fork-tender. Turn tongue several times during cooking.

6. Fifteen minutes before end of cooking time, add cornstarch combined with 1 tablespoon water. Cook 15 minutes longer, until sauce is slightly thickened. Add pears; heat through.

7. To serve, slice tongue, and arrange down center of serving platter. Surround with sauce and pear halves.

Makes 6 servings.

Tongue with Sweet-and-Sour Sauce

1 (4- to 5-pound size) smoked beef tongue	1 cup cider vinegar
2 small onions	½ cup golden raisins
2 bay leaves	½ cup crushed gingersnaps
12 whole black peppercorns	6 thin lemon slices
1 tablespoon salt	1 small onion, thinly sliced
	1 bay leaf
	½ teaspoon salt

Sauce
1½ cups dark-brown sugar,
   firmly packed

1. In large kettle, cover tongue with cold water. Add 2 onions, 2 bay leaves, peppercorns, and salt.

2. Bring to boiling. Reduce heat; simmer, covered, 4 hours, or until tongue is tender.

3. Meanwhile, make Sauce: In medium-size saucepan, combine sugar with vinegar and ¾ cup water.

4. Add raisins, gingersnaps, lemon slices, onion slices, bay leaf, and salt, mixing well. Over medium heat, bring to boiling, stirring. Reduce heat; simmer, uncovered, 10 minutes, stirring occasionally.

5. Remove lemon slices and bay leaf; simmer, uncovered, 10 minutes longer.

6. Drain tongue; cool slightly. Trim off root and gristle from thick end. With sharp knife, gently slit skin on underside of tongue, from thick end to tip. Peel off skin, and discard.

7. Cut tongue into slices. Arrange on serving platter. Pour sauce over.

Makes 8 servings.

Hasenpfeffer

1 package (about 2½ pounds) thawed frozen cut-up rabbit	12 whole black peppercorns
2½ teaspoons salt	Parsley sprig
6 tablespoons butter or margarine	½ teaspoon dried thyme leaves
1 medium-size onion	1 bay leaf
4 whole cloves	2 cans (10½-ounce size) condensed beef broth, undiluted
1 cup port	3 tablespoons flour
¼ cup lemon juice	
	Currant jelly

1. Preheat oven to 350°F.

2. Rinse rabbit in cold water; pat dry with paper towels. Rub with 1½ teaspoons salt.

3. In 3 tablespoons hot butter in skillet, sauté rabbit until browned on all sides—about 20 minutes. As pieces brown, remove to 3-quart casserole.

4. Add onion stuck with cloves, port, and lemon juice to casserole. Add peppercorns, parsley, thyme, and bay leaf, tied in cheesecloth bag.

5. Pour in beef broth; bake, covered, 1½ hours. Discard onion and cheesecloth bag.

6. Make gravy: In small saucepan, melt rest of butter; remove from heat. Stir in flour until smooth.

7. Gradually stir in stock from rabbit (you should have about 3½ cups); bring to boil, stirring; cook a few more minutes, till thickened. Taste; add rest of salt, if desired.

8. Serve rabbit, with some of gravy poured over it, on heated platter. Pass remaining gravy, along with dish of currant jelly.

Makes 4 servings.

POULTRY

Breasts of Chicken Paprika

6 whole chicken breasts (4 pounds)	2 cans (10½-ounce size) condensed chicken broth, undiluted
4 tablespoons butter or margarine	2 tablespoons paprika
16 small white onions (1 pound)	2 teaspoons salt
1 cup chopped onion	⅓ cup flour
8 small carrots (¾ pound)	½ cup dry white wine
	2 cups dairy sour cream

1. Wash chicken breasts well; pat dry with paper towels. Cut each in half; remove skin, and discard.

2. Brown chicken pieces, half at a time, in 2 tablespoons hot butter in large, heavy skillet or Dutch oven. Remove as browned.

3. In same skillet, sauté whole and chopped onions in remaining 2 tablespoons butter until lightly browned.

4. Cut carrots into 1½-inch pieces. Add to onions; sauté 1 or 2 minutes. Add chicken broth, paprika, and salt, stirring until paprika is dissolved.

5. Return chicken to skillet, overlapping pieces; bring to boiling. Reduce heat; simmer, covered, 15 minutes. Rearrange chicken so top pieces are on bottom, for more even cooking. Simmer, covered, 25 minutes longer, or until all chicken pieces are tender.

6. Remove chicken to heated serving platter; keep warm.

7. In small bowl, blend flour with wine to make a smooth paste. Stir into hot liquid in skillet until smooth. (You should have about 3½ cups liquid.)

8. Bring to boiling, stirring. Reduce heat; simmer 2 minutes.

9. Remove from heat. Slowly stir in sour cream; heat gently 1 or 2 minutes, but do not boil.

10. Pour sauce over chicken. Garnish with parsley sprigs, if you wish.

Makes 8 to 10 servings.

Note: If desired, prepare chicken ahead; freeze before adding sour cream. To serve, thaw in refrigerator; reheat gently, and add sour cream.

Poached Chicken and Winter Vegetables

2 (2-pound size) ready-to-cook whole broiler–fryers	½ cup dry white wine
Salt	½ teaspoon dried thyme leaves
Pepper	1 pound small new potatoes
¼ cup butter or margarine	1 can (1 pound) whole carrots, drained
8 leeks	¼ cup butter or margarine
1 small head (1 pound) green cabbage	1 tablespoon snipped chives
1 can (10½ ounces) condensed chicken broth, undiluted	

1. Rinse chickens well; dry with paper towels. Sprinkle inside of each with ½ teaspoon salt and ⅛ teaspoon pepper. Tuck wings under body; fasten skin at neck with skewer.

2. In ¼ cup hot butter in Dutch oven, over medium heat, brown chicken well all over—about 10 minutes. Turn carefully with two wooden spoons; do not break skin.

3. Meanwhile, trim leeks. Cut off root ends and green stems—leeks should be 7 inches long after trimming. Wash thoroughly. Wash cabbage; remove core. Cut cabbage into sixths; set aside.

4. Turn chickens breast side up. Add chicken broth and wine. Sprinkle each chicken with ¼ teaspoon salt and ¼ teaspoon thyme. Bring to boiling; reduce heat; simmer, covered, 60 minutes, or until chicken is tender.

5. Meanwhile, in 1 inch boiling salted water in medium-size saucepan, cook potatoes, covered, 20 minutes, or until tender. Drain; keep covered in saucepan.

6. In 1 inch boiling salted water in a large skillet, simmer leeks, cabbage, and carrots, covered, 15 minutes, or just until cabbage is tender. Drain; return to skillet. Keep covered.

7. To serve, carefully remove chickens to heated platter; remove skewers. Arrange potatoes, leeks, cabbage, and carrots around chickens. Dot vegetables with butter; sprinkle with chives.

Makes 6 servings.

Chicken Fricassee with Fluffy Dumplings

2 slices raw bacon
2 whole chicken breasts and 4 chicken legs (3½ to 4 pounds in all)
3 small onions, quartered
4 medium-size carrots, peeled and cut in 2-inch pieces
2 stalks celery, cut in 1-inch pieces
1 can (10½ ounces) condensed chicken broth, undiluted

2 teaspoons salt
½ teaspoon dried rosemary leaves
2 bay leaves
⅛ teaspoon pepper
6 tablespoons flour

Fluffy Dumplings
1 cup buttermilk-biscuit mix
⅓ cup milk

Parsley (optional)

1. In a 6-quart Dutch oven or deep, heavy skillet, sauté bacon until crisp; remove, and set aside.

2. Wash chicken pieces well; pat dry with paper towels. Split breasts in half; then cut again in half crosswise. Cut drumsticks and thighs apart.

3. In hot bacon fat, sauté chicken pieces, a single layer at a time, until lightly browned; return all chicken to pan.

4. Add onion, carrot, celery, chicken broth, salt, rosemary, bay leaves,

pepper, crumbled bacon, and 3 cups water. Bring to boiling over high heat; reduce heat; simmer, covered, 35 minutes, or until chicken and vegetables are tender.

5. With slotted spoon, remove chicken and vegetables to platter. Strain broth into a large bowl; measure broth, and return to pan. (You should have about 5 cups.) Bring broth to boiling.

6. In small bowl, blend flour and ½ cup water until smooth; pour mixture into boiling broth, stirring constantly. Boil 1 minute, or until broth thickens. Return chicken and vegetables to Dutch oven. Bring to boiling, covered.

7. Meanwhile, make Fluffy Dumplings: Prepare biscuit mix with milk as label directs for dumplings.

8. Drop dough by rounded tablespoonfuls onto top of boiling chicken and vegetables. Cook, uncovered, 10 minutes; cover tightly; cook over medium heat (mixture should be bubbling) 15 minutes longer, or until dumplings are puffed and a wooden pick inserted in one comes out clean.

9. Remove from heat. Arrange on large, heated serving platter; garnish with parsley, if desired.

Makes 6 servings.

Duckling in May Wine

1 (4- to 5-pound size) ready-to-cook duckling, cut in serving pieces	1 cup diced cooked ham
	½ cup diced celery
	6 small white onions
Salt	1 cup May Wine
Pepper	1½ tablespoons butter
4 tablespoons olive or salad oil	1½ tablespoons flour

1. Remove skin and excess fat from duckling; sprinkle pieces lightly with salt and pepper.

2. In hot oil in large skillet, sauté duckling until lightly browned on all sides.

3. Add ham, celery, onions, and wine. Simmer, covered, 30 minutes or until tender.

4. Remove duckling to serving platter; keep warm.

5. Mix butter with flour until smooth; stir into drippings in skillet. Bring to boiling, stirring. Lower heat and simmer 5 minutes. Strain if desired.

6. To serve, pour a little sauce over duckling and pass the rest in a sauce boat.

Makes 4 servings.

Roast Turkey

¼ cup butter or margarine	1 large apple
2 cups chopped onion	1 large onion
1 large apple, unpared and chopped	5 slices raw bacon
1 can (1 pound, 11 ounces) sauerkraut	¼ cup butter or margarine, melted
1 medium-size potato, pared and grated	Sautéed Apple Rings (see p. 42)
1 tablespoon caraway seed	Bratwurst (see p. 42)
½ teaspoon salt	
¾ teaspoon pepper	Parsley
1 (6- to 7-pound size) ready-to-cook turkey	

1. Preheat oven to 325°F.

2. Melt ¼ cup butter in large skillet. Add chopped onion and chopped apple; sauté 10 minutes. Add sauerkraut, grated potato, caraway seed, salt, and ½ teaspoon pepper.

3. Bring to boiling; reduce heat; simmer, uncovered, 5 minutes.

4. Meanwhile, remove giblets and neck from turkey; wash, and set aside. Wash turkey thoroughly inside and out. Pat dry with paper towels. Remove and discard any excess fat.

5. Core apple; cut into wedges. Peel onion, and cut into wedges.

6. Place some apple and onion wedges in neck cavity. Bring skin of neck over back, and fasten with poultry pin.

7. Stuff body cavity with remaining apple and onion wedges, heart, and cut-up gizzard. Omit liver and neck. Close body cavity with poultry pins; lace with twine. Tie ends of legs together; bend wing tips under body.

8. Turn sauerkraut mixture into shallow roasting pan. Place turkey, breast side up, on sauerkraut. Sprinkle ¼ teaspoon pepper over turkey. Place bacon slices evenly over turkey. Insert meat thermometer in inside of thigh at thickest part.

9. Roast turkey, uncovered, 1½ hours. Remove bacon from turkey; add to sauerkraut. Brush turkey with some of melted butter.

10. Roast, uncovered and brushing occasionally with remaining melted butter, 1 hour and 15 minutes longer, or until meat thermometer registers 185°F. Leg joint should move freely.

11. Remove turkey from roasting pan to heated serving platter; remove twine and poultry pins. Turkey should stand in warm place 20 minutes before carving. Keep sauerkraut warm in oven in roasting pan. Meanwhile, prepare Sautéed Apple Rings and Bratwurst, if desired.

12. To serve, remove bacon from sauerkraut, and discard. Gently stir sauerkraut. Remove with slotted spoon, and place around turkey. Arrange Sautéed Apple Rings and Bratwurst around turkey. Garnish with parsley.

Makes 6 servings.

Sautéed Apple Rings

3 large apples

3 tablespoons butter or margarine

1. Core apples; cut each crosswise into 4 rings.
2. Heat butter and sauté apple rings, turning once, just until tender— 4 to 5 minutes. Keep warm. Serve with Roast Turkey.

Bratwurst

1 tablespoon butter or margarine

1 pound bratwurst

1. Sauté bratwurst in butter, turning frequently, until well browned— 20 to 25 minutes.
2. Keep warm. Serve with Roast Turkey.

Makes 6 servings.

Pork & Sausage

Our national snack, the hot dog, originated in Germany. It can still be found there, but it occupies a relatively humble place since it must compete with dozens of other similarly shaped sausages, some fatter and milder, some longer and spicier, each equally tempting when topped with mustard and placed inside a roll. Hot dogs, salami, and bologna are all considered sausages in Germany. In addition, there are about three hundred other delicious spiced meats, most of them made from pork, many of them ready-cooked, at the pork-and-sausage butcher's shop.

The German sausage butcher is a master of his culinary art. He knows how to fill the sausage casings with just the right proportions of different meats, fat, and seasonings, and how to form the sausages into many varied shapes. Some wursts are preserved or smoked, some are fresh and eaten cold, and others are cooked. Weisswurst, for example, is a white, delicately flavored veal sausage, whereas bauernwurst, "the farmer's sausage," is a coarsely ground, smoked pork sausage. Other popular varieties include bratwurst, bockwurst, blutwurst, mettwurst, and leberwurst (liverwurst).

The Germans have been eating pork for centuries; they have helped to spread its popularity through central Europe. In years past, the pork came from wild boars, which were roasted whole on a spit over an open fire. Sometimes the belly of the boar was stuffed with delicacies; for instance, little birds or fish. This custom has disappeared, and instead, tasty side dishes are cooked and eaten as accompaniments to the meat. Pork with cabbage, or sauerkraut, or apples, or even knackwurst sausage are delicious modern German pork specialties.

PORK

Ham Baked in May Wine

1 (12- to 14-pound size) fully-cooked ham	½ cup brown sugar
4 cups May Wine	¼ cup apricot preserves, heated
Dash mace	1 cup canned chicken broth
Whole cloves	3 tablespoons cornstarch
1 cup apricot nectar	3 tablespoons lemon juice
1 jar (12 ounces) honey	

1. Preheat oven to 350°F.

2. Place ham in a deep roasting pan.   Bake, uncovered, 40 minutes.

2. Meanwhile, in hot butter in medium-size skillet, sauté onions with mace.   Bake 1 hour and 50 minutes longer, basting frequently.

4. Carefully remove rind from ham; score fat into diamond pattern; insert a clove in each diamond.   Pour 1 cup wine, the apricot nectar, and honey over ham.   Insert meat thermometer in center, away from bone.   Bake 45 minutes longer, basting several times.

5. Spread brown sugar over top of ham; brush with apricot preserves. Bake 15 minutes longer or until internal temperature is 155°F. on meat thermometer.

6. Remove ham to serving platter.   Let stand about 20 minutes before carving.

7. Meanwhile, pour pan drippings into medium-size saucepan.   Add remaining wine and chicken broth; bring to boiling, skimming off fat on top.   Mix cornstarch with ¼ cup cold water until smooth; gradually stir into wine mixture.   Bring to boiling, stirring; boil 3 minutes.   Stir in lemon juice; keep warm.   Serve with ham.

Makes about 24 servings.

Fresh-Ham Hocks, Country Style

5 pounds fresh-ham hocks	Pepper
1 quart apple cider	4 cups cubed (1 inch) yellow turnip or rutabaga (1½ pounds)
¼ cup cider vinegar	
¼ cup butter or margarine	
3 cups sliced onion	1 bay leaf
1 teaspoon sugar	1 jar (1 pound) applesauce
Salt	

1. Preheat oven to 350°F. Wash ham hocks; dry with paper towels. Arrange in 15- by 10- by 2-inch roasting pan. Pour cider and vinegar over ham hocks. Cover pan with foil; bake 1½ hours, basting several times with liquid.

2. Meanwhile, in hot butter in medium-size skillet, sauté onion with sugar until onion is lightly browned. Sprinkle with ½ teaspoon salt and ⅛ teaspoon pepper; set aside.

3. Remove ham hocks from oven; skim off fat, and discard. Add turnip; sprinkle with 1½ teaspoons salt and ½ teaspoon pepper. Add browned onion and bay leaf; bake, covered, 1½ hours.

4. Remove foil; spoon applesauce around ham hocks; bake, uncovered, ½ hour longer, or until ham hocks are very tender. Serve with turnips and pan liquid spooned over all.

Makes 6 servings.

Pork Chops with Cabbage

8 rib pork chops, about 1 inch thick (3 pounds)	1 teaspoon seasoned salt
2 tablespoons butter or margarine	2 tablespoons chopped parsley
¼ cup chopped onion	**Braised Cabbage**
1 teaspoon salt	1 head cabbage (2½ pounds)
¼ teaspoon pepper	¼ cup butter or margarine
½ teaspoon dried thyme leaves	1½ teaspoons seasoned salt
1 bay leaf	2 tablespoons white-wine vinegar
2 sprigs parsley	
	1 tablespoon flour
Parsley Potatoes	1 tablespoon white-wine vinegar
2 pounds small new potatoes	
¼ cup butter or margarine, melted	

1. Wipe pork chops with damp paper towels. Trim off fat, if necessary. In 2 tablespoons hot butter in Dutch oven, brown chops on both sides—about 20 minutes in all.

2. Sprinkle chops with onion, salt, pepper, and thyme. Add bay leaf, parsley sprigs, and 2 tablespoons water. Simmer, covered, 45 to 50 minutes, or until chops are tender.

3. Meanwhile, make Parsley Potatoes: In 1 inch boiling water in medium-size saucepan, cook potatoes, covered, until tender—about 20 minutes. Drain; remove skins. Return potatoes to saucepan. Add melted butter, 1 teaspoon seasoned salt, and the chopped parsley; toss lightly. Keep warm.

4. Make Braised Cabbage: Shred cabbage finely—there should be 3 quarts. Heat ¼ cup butter in large skillet. Add cabbage, and toss to coat well with the butter. Add 1½ teaspoons seasoned salt and 2 tablespoons vinegar; cook over medium heat, covered, 10 minutes, or until cabbage is just tender. Remove from heat; keep covered until needed.

5. To serve, mound cabbage in center of large platter; stand chops around the cabbage, overlapping slightly. (Discard bay leaf and parsley sprigs.) Arrange potatoes around edge. Keep warm.

6. Heat drippings in Dutch oven to boiling. Mix flour with 1 tablespoon vinegar and 2 tablespoons water until smooth. Gradually add to drippings; cook, stirring, until thickened. Spoon some of gravy over chops; pass the rest in a small bowl.

Makes 8 servings.

Pork-Chop-and-Potato Scallop

6 shoulder pork chops, ½ inch thick (1¾ pounds)
Flour
1½ teaspoons seasoned salt
Pepper
1½ teaspoons salt
6 medium-size potatoes, pared and thinly sliced (2 pounds)

4 medium-size onions, thinly sliced
1 can (10¾ ounces) condensed Cheddar-cheese soup, undiluted
1½ cups milk

1. Wipe pork chops with damp paper towels. Trim excess fat, and reserve. Combine 3 tablespoons flour, the seasoned salt, and ¼ teaspoon pepper; use to coat chops.

2. Heat fat trimmed from chops in a skillet. Add chops, and brown well on both sides—about 20 minutes in all.

3. Preheat oven to 350°F.

4. Meanwhile, combine 2 tablespoons flour, the salt, and ¼ teaspoon pepper. Arrange half of potato slices and half of onion slices in a 3-quart shallow baking dish; sprinkle with half of flour mixture. Add remaining potato, onion, and flour mixture.

5. In small saucepan, combine soup and milk; heat just to boiling, stirring until smooth. Pour over potato mixture in baking dish. Arrange browned chops on top. Cover dish with foil.

6. Bake, covered, 30 minutes. Remove foil; bake 1 hour longer, or just until potatoes are tender.

Makes 6 servings.

Pork Chops, Rhinelander Style

6 loin pork chops, about 1
   inch thick (2¼ pounds)
½ teaspoon salt
¼ teaspoon pepper
¼ teaspoon dried thyme leaves
2 cans (10½-ounce size) condensed beef broth, undiluted
4 cups thinly sliced pared
   apple

1 cup coarsely chopped onion
1¾ pounds potatoes, pared
   and quartered
12 link sausages (about ¾
   pound)

Parsley sprigs

1. Wipe pork chops with damp paper towels. Trim a small amount of fat from chops.

2. In large skillet, slowly heat fat from chops. Add chops; sauté slowly until nicely browned on both sides—about 15 minutes.

3. Sprinkle salt, pepper, and thyme over chops. Add ½ cup beef broth; simmer over low heat, covered, until chops are tender—45 to 50 minutes.   Add water if necessary.

4. Meanwhile, in 4-quart kettle, bring rest of beef broth to boiling. Add apple, onion, and potatoes; bring back to boiling. Reduce heat, and simmer, covered, until potatoes are tender and bouillon is absorbed— about 30 minutes.   Uncover last 5 minutes.

5. In medium-size skillet, sauté sausages, turning until browned all over and cooked through—about 30 minutes. Drain on paper towels; keep warm.

6. Taste apple-potato mixture for seasoning; add salt if needed. Mound in center of round platter. Arrange pork chops and sausage around apple mixture.   Garnish with parsley.

Makes 6 servings.

Pork with Caraway Sauerkraut

2 tablespoons butter or
   margarine
¼ cup light-brown sugar, firmly
   packed
1½ cups sliced unpared tart
   cooking apples
½ cup coarsely chopped onion
1 cup leftover pork gravy or
   canned chicken gravy

1 can (16 ounces) sauerkraut,
   drained
½ teaspoon salt
1 teaspoon caraway seed
8 cooked roast-pork slices,
   about ⅛ inch thick

1. In large skillet with tight-fitting lid, combine butter with sugar; cook, stirring, over low heat, until sugar melts.

2. Add apples and onion, mixing well; simmer the mixture, covered, 5 minutes.

3. Stir in gravy, sauerkraut, salt, and caraway seed; bring to boiling. Reduce heat. Arrange pork slices on top; simmer, covered, 10 minutes longer.

Makes 6 servings.

Pork-and-Sauerkraut Goulash

1 (2-pound size) boneless pork shoulder roast, trimmed
2 cups chopped onion
1 clove garlic, finely chopped
1 teaspoon dried dillweed
1 teaspoon caraway seed
1 tablespoon salt
1 beef bouillon cube

½ cup boiling water
1 tablespoon paprika
1 can (1 pound, 11 ounces) sauerkraut, drained
2 cups dairy sour cream

Hot boiled new potatoes

1. Wipe meat with damp paper towels. Cut meat into 1½-inch cubes; discard fat.

2. In large Dutch oven or heavy skillet, combine pork, onion, garlic, dill, caraway seed, salt, bouillon cube, and boiling water; bring to boiling. Reduce heat; simmer, covered, 1 hour.

3. Stir in paprika until dissolved.

4. Add sauerkraut; mix well. Simmer, covered, 1 hour longer, or until meat is tender.

5. Remove from heat. Gradually stir in sour cream. Return to heat until heated through. Do not let boil. Serve with boiled new potatoes, peeled.

Makes 6 servings.

Pork Hocks and Sauerkraut

6 fresh-pork hocks
1 teaspoon poultry seasoning
⅓ cup grated onion
¼ teaspoon caraway seed
1 teaspoon salt
2 tablespoons butter or margarine

2 tablespoons sugar
1 tablespoon white vinegar
1¼ cups grated pared potato
1 cup grated pared apple
1 can (1 pound, 11 ounces) sauerkraut, undrained

1. Singe pork hocks, if necessary. Wash; drain on paper towels.

2. Place hocks in 6-quart Dutch oven; add poultry seasoning, 2 tablespoons onion, the caraway seed, ½ teaspoon salt, and 3 cups water; bring to boiling. Reduce heat, and simmer, covered, 2½ to 3 hours, or until meat is tender.

3. Melt butter in large, deep skillet. Stir in sugar, vinegar, potato, apple, and remaining salt and onion. Sauté, stirring, about 3 minutes. Add sauerkraut with its liquid.

4. Drain pork hocks. Place on top of sauerkraut; simmer, covered, 30 minutes.

5. To serve, drain sauerkraut, and place on heated platter. Arrange pork hocks on top.

Makes 6 servings.

Glazed Smoked Pork Butt

1 (3- to 3½-pound size) bone- less smoked pork butt	6 medium-size carrots
4 whole black peppercorns	6 medium-size white turnips
2 whole cloves	¼ cup orange marmalade
1 head cabbage (about 2 pounds)	2 teaspoons prepared mustard
	Chopped parsley

1. Place pork butt in an 8-quart kettle. Add peppercorns, cloves, and water to cover. Bring to boiling; reduce heat; simmer 2¼ hours (45 minutes per pound), or until pork is fork-tender.

2. Meanwhile, remove outer leaves from cabbage; cut cabbage into 6 wedges. Pare carrots and turnips; cut turnips in half. Add vegetables to pork during last half hour of cooking.

3. Remove pork from kettle; remove net covering or string.

4. In small bowl, blend marmalade and mustard. Spread over pork.

5. Run pork under broiler, 3 or 4 inches from heat, 2 to 3 minutes, or until richly glazed.

6. Arrange pork and vegetables on large, heated serving platter. Sprinkle turnips with chopped parsley.

Makes 6 servings.

Sauerkraut and Pork

2 onions	4 cans (1-pound size) sauer- kraut (2 quarts), drained
8 whole cloves	
2 carrots, pared	1 tablespoon butter or margarine

2 pounds unsliced raw bacon,
  halved
	2 cans (14-ounce size) clear
	  chicken broth (3½ cups)

1 (2-pound size) smoked bone- less pork butt	1 cup white wine
10 whole black peppercorns	¼ cup lemon juice
6 juniper berries (optional)	

1. Stud each onion with 4 cloves. Put onions, carrots, bacon, and smoked butt in large kettle.

2. Add peppercorns and berries, tied in cheesecloth bag. Cover with sauerkraut. Add butter.

3. Combine chicken broth, wine, and lemon juice. Pour over mixture in kettle; bring to boiling point.

4. Reduce heat; simmer, covered, 1½ to 2 hours, or until butt is tender when pierced with fork. Discard onions and cheesecloth bag.

5. To serve, cut each piece of bacon into 4 slices, butt into 8 slices. Arrange on large platter, with sauerkraut. Slice carrots crosswise, and use as garnish.

Makes 6 to 8 servings.

Smoked Loin of Pork

1 (5-pound size) smoked loin of pork (12 ribs)	1½ cups sliced pared apple
2 whole bay leaves	¼ cup light-brown sugar, packed
8 whole allspice	1 bay leaf, crushed
6 whole black peppercorns	2 cans (1-pound, 11-ounce size) sauerkraut, drained
6 slices raw bacon, cut into ½-inch pieces	1 cup dry white wine
1½ cups chopped onion	

1. Wipe pork loin with damp paper towels.

2. In large kettle, place pork, 2 quarts water, 2 bay leaves, the allspice, and peppercorns. If necessary, cut pork loin in half to fit in kettle.

3. Bring to boiling; reduce heat, and simmer, covered, 1 hour. Remove from heat. Let pork stand in liquid in kettle until ready to bake.

4. Preheat oven to 350°F.

5. Meanwhile, in 15½- by 10½- by 2¼-inch baking pan, cook bacon, onion, apple over medium heat, stirring, until onion is soft—about 10 minutes.

6. Add brown sugar, crushed bay leaf, sauerkraut, wine, and 1 cup of liquid from pork loin. Cook, uncovered, stirring frequently, over medium heat 20 minutes.

7. Place pork loin in center of baking pan on top of sauerkraut. Baste pork with some of liquid from sauerkraut. Bake, uncovered, 30 minutes, to glaze pork.

8. Baste pork again. Cover pan tightly with foil; bake 40 minutes.

9. To serve, slice pork loin into chops; serve with sauerkraut and boiled potatoes or Potato Pancakes (see p. 23).

Makes 8 to 10 servings.

Loin of Pork with Knackwurst, Sauerkraut, and Potatoes

1 (3-pound size) loin of pork	½ cup dry white wine
3 cans (1-pound size)	4 medium-size knackwurst
sauerkraut, drained	8 small white potatoes, pared
3 cloves garlic, crushed	(1½ pounds)
¼ teaspoon pepper	
½ teaspoon caraway seed	¼ cup chopped parsley

1. Preheat oven to 325°F.

2. Wipe pork with damp paper towels. Place pork, fat side up, in shallow roasting pan. (Omit rack; pork will rest on bones.) Insert meat thermometer into center of meaty part of pork; it should not rest against bone.

3. Roast pork 2½ hours, or to 185°F. on meat thermometer. Remove to heated platter; keep warm.

4. While pork is roasting: In 2-quart casserole, combine sauerkraut, garlic, pepper, caraway seed, and wine; toss lightly to combine. Bake, covered, 1 hour.

5. With sharp knife, slash each knackwurst twice. Arrange over sauerkraut; bake, covered, 40 minutes longer.

6. In large saucepan, cover potatoes with boiling water; cook, covered, 25 to 30 minutes, or until tender. Drain.

7. To serve, place pork loin in center of warm platter. Surround with sauerkraut. Arrange potatoes and knackwurst around sauerkraut. Sprinkle potatoes with parsley.

Makes 8 servings.

Pork Meatball Casserole with Sour-Cream Sauce

Potato Border	½ teaspoon dried marjoram
1 package (2 envelopes)	leaves
instant mashed potato	¼ teaspoon pepper
¼ cup butter or margarine	2 tablespoons flour
2 teaspoons salt	2 tablespoons salad oil
1 cup milk	
	Sour-Cream Sauce
Meatballs	2 tablespoons flour
1½ pounds lean ground pork	1 beef bouillon cube
1 egg	½ cup dairy sour cream
½ cup packaged seasoned dry	2 teaspoons lemon juice
bread crumbs	
½ cup milk	¼ cup grated Parmesan cheese
½ cup finely chopped onion	Parsley
1½ teaspoons salt	

1. Make Potato Border: Prepare both envelopes mashed potato as package label directs, using amount of water specified on package and the amounts of butter, salt, and milk listed above. Set aside.

2. Make Meatballs: In large bowl, combine pork, egg, bread crumbs, milk, onion, salt, marjoram, and pepper; mix lightly until well blended. Shape into balls about 1½ inches in diameter.

3. Preheat oven to 350°F. Roll meatballs in flour, coating completely.

4. In hot oil in skillet, sauté meatballs until browned on all sides. Remove, as they brown, to a 2-quart casserole or shallow baking dish; mound in center.

5. Make Sour-Cream Sauce: Measure drippings in skillet; add more oil, if necessary, to make 2 tablespoons. Return to skillet; stir in flour until smooth. Gradually stir in 1 cup water and the bouillon cube.

6. Bring to boiling. Remove from heat. Add sour cream and lemon juice, stirring to combine; simmer 2 minutes. Remove from heat.

7. Spoon mashed potato around meatballs in casserole; sprinkle potato with cheese. Pour sauce over meatballs.

8. Bake, uncovered, 1 hour, or until potato is golden brown. Garnish with parsley.

Makes 8 servings.

Spareribs and Sauerkraut Baked in Cider

2 racks spareribs, with center bones cracked (about 3 pounds)	1 cup pared, thinly sliced apples
1 teaspoon salt	1 teaspoon caraway seed
¼ teaspoon pepper	2 cups apple cider
1 pound sauerkraut, drained	1 tablespoon light-brown sugar

1. Preheat oven to 350°F.

2. Wipe ribs with damp paper towels; sprinkle with salt and pepper. Place ribs, fat side down, on rack in shallow roasting pan.

3. Bake, uncovered, 30 minutes. Pour off drippings. Turn ribs; bake 20 minutes longer.

4. On one rack of spareribs, spread drained sauerkraut; then layer with apple slices, and sprinkle with caraway seed. Pour over ¾ cup cider. Cover with second rack of ribs; fasten with skewers.

5. Cover pan loosely with foil. Bake covered, 1½ hours, basting several times with ¾ cup of remaining cider.

6. Uncover pan; baste with rest of cider. Sprinkle top of ribs with sugar.

7. Bake, uncovered, 30 minutes, or until nicely browned, basting occasionally with pan juice.

8. To serve, remove to heated platter. With kitchen shears, cut crosswise, through both rib sections, into serving pieces.

Makes 4 or 5 servings.

SAUSAGE

Bratwurst with Paprika Sauce

1½ pounds bratwurst

Paprika Sauce
2 tablespoons butter or
   margarine
2 tablespoons finely chopped
   shallots
2 tablespoons flour

1 tablespoon paprika
¼ teaspoon salt
Dash garlic powder
1 chicken bouillon cube
½ cup dairy sour cream

Finely chopped parsley

1. Cover bratwurst with hot water; bring to boiling. Remove from heat; let stand in hot water 5 minutes.

2. Drain bratwurst. Arrange on rack in broiler pan; broil, 6 inches from heat, about 8 minutes on each side, or until golden.

3. Meanwhile, make Paprika Sauce: In hot butter in medium-size saucepan, sauté shallots until golden—3 to 5 minutes.

4. Remove from heat. Stir in flour, paprika, salt, and garlic powder. Then stir in bouillon cube, dissolved in 1 cup boiling water, until smooth.

5. Bring to boiling. Reduce heat; simmer 5 minutes, stirring occasionally. Remove from heat. Stir in sour cream.

6. To serve, pour sauce over bratwurst. Sprinkle with parsley.

Makes 4 servings.

Kielbasa with Red Cabbage

¼ cup light-brown sugar,
   firmly packed
1 tablespoon grated orange
   peel
1 clove garlic, crushed
1½ teaspoons salt
½ teaspoon nutmeg
¼ teaspoon pepper
⅛ teaspoon ground cloves

1 (2-pound) head red cabbage,
   shredded (about 12 cups)
3 medium-size onions, sliced
3 medium-size cooking apples,
   pared, cored, and sliced
1 large red pepper, cut into
   thin strips
½ cup orange juice
¼ cup red-wine vinegar
1 ring (2 pounds) kielbasa

1. Preheat oven to 350°F. In small bowl, combine brown sugar, orange peel, garlic, salt, nutmeg, pepper, and cloves.

2. In Dutch oven, arrange in layers half of cabbage, half of onion, and half of apple; sprinkle with half of brown-sugar mixture; add half of pepper strips.   Repeat.

3. Pour orange juice and vinegar over top.

4. Bake, covered, 1 hour.

5. Make ¼-inch-deep slashes, at 2-inch intervals, in kielbasa.   Place in Dutch oven, pressing down to partially cover kielbasa with pan juices. Bake, covered, 30 minutes.

Makes 6 servings.

Knackwurst in Beer

Knackwurst in Beer	Glazed Baked Beans
4 knackwurst	2 cans (1-pound size) pork
1 medium-size onion, sliced	and beans
1 clove garlic, halved	2 tablespoons butter or
1 cup beer	margarine
	⅓ cup brown sugar

1. About 4 hours before cooking, prepare Knackwurst in Beer: Slash each knackwurst, diagonally, at 1-inch intervals.   Place in a medium-size bowl.   Top with onion and garlic; pour beer over all.   Refrigerate, covered.

2. About ½ hour before dinner, make Glazed Baked Beans: Turn beans into small skillet.   Cook over medium heat, covered, until heated through—about 20 minutes.   Remove from heat.   Dot with butter; sprinkle brown sugar evenly over top.   (If necessary, wrap handle of skillet with foil.)   Broil beans, 2 inches from heat, until sugar is melted and bubbling—about 2 minutes.

3. Meanwhile, lift knackwurst out of onion-beer mixture; set both aside, discarding garlic.

4. Sauté knackwurst in skillet until nicely browned.   Add onion-beer mixture, and simmer, covered, 8 minutes.   Simmer, uncovered, until most of liquid has evaporated.

5. Serve beans with knackwurst and onions.

Makes 3 or 4 servings.

Frankfurter Salad Bowl

1 package (9 ounces) frozen French-style green beans	1 clove garlic, crushed
1 pound frankfurters	1½ teaspoons salt
3 tablespoons olive or salad oil	¼ teaspoon pepper
1 cup sliced onion	½ teaspoon dried oregano leaves
1 cup thinly sliced celery	⅓ cup tarragon vinegar
½ cup green-pepper strips	½ cup packaged croutons

1. Cook beans as package label directs; drain.

2. Cut frankfurters into 1-inch pieces. In hot oil in medium-size skillet, sauté frankfurters until golden—about 5 minutes.

3. Combine beans and frankfurters with onion, celery, green pepper, garlic, salt, pepper, oregano, and vinegar; toss to combine.

4. Refrigerate until well chilled—about 2 hours. Just before serving, toss salad with croutons.

Makes 4 to 6 servings.

Sausage, Apple, and Cabbage Casserole

1 pound link sausage	1 can (1 pound, 4 ounces)
3 tablespoons flour	apple slices, undrained
1 small head green cabbage	⅓ cup light-brown sugar,
(1½ pounds), finely	firmly packed
shredded	⅓ cup cider vinegar
	1 teaspoon salt

1. Lightly coat sausage with flour. In large skillet, over low heat, sauté until browned on all sides. Drain well on paper towels.

2. Preheat oven to 375°F.

3. In 2-quart casserole, place half the cabbage, all of sausage, then apple slices and any liquid. Top with rest of cabbage.

4. Combine brown sugar, vinegar, salt, and ¼ cup water in small saucepan; bring to boiling, stirring.

5. Pour over mixture in casserole; bake, covered, 20 to 30 minutes, or until cabbage is tender but still crisp. If desired, serve with Caraway Noodles (see p. 22).

Makes 4 servings.

Pork-and-Apple Meat Loaf

2 pounds ground chuck	1 can (1 pound, 4 ounces)
1 pound pork sausage meat	sliced apples, undrained and
¾ cup chopped green pepper	coarsely chopped
⅔ cup chopped onion	1 teaspoon salt
1 egg	¼ teaspoon pepper

Gingersnap Sauce (see p. 56)

1. Preheat oven to 325°F.

2. Combine all ingredients, except sauce, in large bowl; toss gently to mix well.

3. Pack mixture firmly into a 9- by 5- by 3-inch loaf pan.

4. Invert loaf pan over well-greased, shallow baking pan; unmold meat-loaf mixture.

5. Bake 1½ hours, brushing occasionally with pan drippings.

6. With wide spatula, remove meat loaf to serving platter. To serve, cut crosswise into slices. Serve with Gingersnap Sauce.

Makes 8 servings.

Gingersnap Sauce

2 slices raw bacon
¼ cup finely chopped onion
⅓ cup gingersnap crumbs
  (about 6 gingersnaps)
¼ cup red-wine vinegar

¼ cup light-brown sugar, firmly
  packed
1 can (10½ ounces) con-
  densed beef broth, undiluted

1. In medium-size saucepan, sauté bacon until crisp. Drain on paper towels. Crumble, and set aside.

2. Drain off all but 1 tablespoon drippings from skillet. In drippings, sauté onion, stirring, until tender.

3. Add gingersnap crumbs, vinegar, brown sugar, and beef broth.

4. Bring to boiling, stirring. Reduce heat; simmer 5 minutes, stirring occasionally.

5. Remove from heat. Add bacon. Serve hot, over Pork-and-Apple Meat Loaf.

Makes about 1½ cups.

Desserts

No matter how large a German dinner has been, no one would ever think of skipping dessert. The meal is always topped off by the *süsse Speisen,* or sweet dishes. They may be custards sweetened with fruits or liqueurs, or fresh-fruit pancakes or dumplings, or they may be dishes made of rice or tapioca.

Whipped-cream desserts, like the Bavarian creams here, are extremely popular in Germany, and frequently other desserts are crowned with a topping of the delicious white mixture. Puddings are almost as popular in Germany as they are in England. They are steamed for hours in a pudding mold or basin, then served with a fruit sauce. Because German puddings are heavier than their British or French counterparts, they are most appropriate after a light meal.

Macaroon Bavarian Cream

.3 envelopes unflavored gelatin
1¾ cups sugar
2 cups milk
6 egg yolks
4 teaspoons vanilla extract

4 cups crumbled almond macaroons
4 cups heavy cream

Brandied Apricots (see p. 58)

1. Sprinkle gelatin over 1 cup water; let soften.
2. Meanwhile, combine sugar and milk in medium-size saucepan; cook over medium heat, stirring occasionally, just until sugar is dissolved.
3. Add softened gelatin; stir until gelatin is dissolved. Remove from heat.
4. In large bowl, beat egg yolks slightly. Gradually add gelatin mixture, beating constantly. Stir in vanilla and macaroons.

5. Refrigerate until mixture is consistency of unbeaten egg white—about 20 minutes.

6. In large bowl, beat cream until stiff. Using wire whip or rubber scraper, fold in thickened gelatin mixture.

7. Pour into a 3½-quart mold, which has been rinsed in cold water. Refrigerate, covered, overnight.

8. Make Brandied Apricots.

9. To serve, run spatula around edge of mold, to loosen. Invert onto serving plate. Place hot towel over mold; shake several times to release. Garnish with Brandied Apricots.

Makes 12 servings.

Brandied Apricots

2 cans (1-pound, 12-ounce size) whole apricots	⅓ cup brandy

1. Drain apricots, reserving ½ cup syrup.

2. In medium-size bowl, combine apricots, reserved syrup, and brandy.

3. Refrigerate, covered, overnight. Serve with Macaroon Bavarian Cream.

Makes 12 servings.

Strawberries on Strawberry Bavarian Cream

4 pint boxes strawberries	2 envelopes unflavored gelatin
1 tablespoon lemon juice	2 cups heavy cream
1 cup sugar	
Red food coloring	Fresh mint sprigs

1. Gently wash strawberries under cold water; drain well. Hull.

2. Crush half the strawberries with potato masher, or blend in electric blender 1 minute. You should have about 2 cups purée.

3. In large bowl, combine crushed strawberries, lemon juice, sugar, and a few drops food coloring; stir until well blended.

4. In small saucepan, sprinkle gelatin over ½ cup cold water to soften. Heat, over low heat, stirring constantly, until gelatin is dissolved. Stir gelatin into the strawberry mixture.

5. Place bowl in larger bowl of ice and water. Chill, stirring occasionally, until mixture thickens and mounds slightly.

6. Meanwhile, in large bowl, with electric mixer, beat cream until stiff. Carefully fold chilled gelatin mixture into cream.

7. Turn mixture into a 2-quart shallow glass serving bowl; refrigerate at least 4 hours, or until it is firm.

8. To serve, mound remaining whole strawberries on Bavarian Cream. Decorate with sprigs of fresh mint.

Makes 8 to 10 servings.

Strawberries in May Wine Bowl

½ cup dried Waldmeister or woodruff	4 quarts Moselle or Rhine wine
1 cup boiling water	Ice
2 cups confectioners' sugar	2 quarts chilled champagne or club soda
1 cup cognac	1 cup fresh strawberries

1. Place dried herbs in small bowl; add boiling water. Let stand 1 hour; strain. Place 3 tablespoons in punch bowl.

2. Stir in sugar, cognac, and wine; add ice.

3. Just before serving, pour in champagne or soda and float strawberries in the bowl.

Makes 10 to 15 servings.

Apple Pancakes

1 cup sifted all-purpose flour	3 tablespoons butter or margarine, melted
2 teaspoons baking powder	
½ teaspoon salt	1 cup pared, thinly sliced apple
2 tablespoons sugar	
1 egg	Soft butter
1 cup milk	Sour-Cream Topping (see below)

1. Sift flour with baking powder, salt, and sugar into medium-size bowl.

2. With rotary beater, beat egg. Add milk and butter; beat until well mixed.

3. Pour into dry ingredients; beat only until combined—batter will be lumpy. Stir in apple.

4. Meanwhile, slowly heat griddle or heavy skillet. To test temperature, drop a little cold water onto hot griddle; water should roll off in drops.

5. Use about ¼ cup batter for each pancake; cook until bubbles form on surface and edges become dry. Turn; cook 2 minutes longer, or until nicely browned on underside. Serve with soft butter and Sour-Cream Topping.

Makes 8 (4-inch) pancakes.

Sour-Cream Topping

1½ cups dairy sour cream	2 tablespoons light-brown sugar
2 tablespoons honey	
	⅛ teaspoon nutmeg

1. Combine all ingredients in small bowl; blend thoroughly.
2. Serve at room temperature with Apple Pancakes.
Makes 1⅔ cups.

Sour-Cream Pancakes

1 cup sifted all-purpose flour	2 eggs
½ teaspoon baking powder	3 tablespoons butter or
½ teaspoon baking soda	margarine, melted
½ teaspoon salt	
½ cup dairy sour cream	Soft butter
½ cup milk	Spicy Applesauce (see below)

1. Sift flour with baking powder, baking soda, and salt. Combine sour cream and milk, stirring well.
2. In large bowl of electric mixer, at high speed, beat eggs until light and fluffy.
3. At low speed, alternately blend in flour mixture and sour-cream mixture, beginning and ending with flour. Then blend in melted butter.
4. Meanwhile, slowly heat griddle or heavy skillet. To test temperature, drop a little cold water onto hot griddle; water should roll off in drops.
5. Use a scant ¼ cup batter for each pancake; cook until bubbles form on surface and edges become dry. Turn; cook 2 minutes longer, or until nicely browned on underside. Serve with soft butter and Spicy Applesauce.
Makes 9 (4-inch) pancakes.

Spicy Applesauce

1 can (1 pound) applesauce	½ teaspoon nutmeg
1 tablespoon butter or	½ teaspoon cinnamon
margarine	

1. Combine all ingredients in small bowl; blend thoroughly.
2. Serve warm or cold with Sour-Cream Pancakes.
Makes 1⅓ cups.

Steamed Apple Pudding

1½ cups sifted all-purpose flour	¼ teaspoon ground cloves
1 teaspoon baking soda	¼ cup butter or margarine,
½ teaspoon salt	softened
½ teaspoon cinnamon	1 cup sugar
½ teaspoon nutmeg	2 eggs, well beaten

4 medium-size apples, pared   ½ cup dark raisins
   and shredded (about 2⅓
   cups)   Light cream

1. Grease well a 1½-quart, heat-proof bowl.

2. Into small bowl, sift flour with baking soda, salt, and spices; set aside.

3. In large bowl, with wooden spoon, beat butter, sugar, and eggs until mixture is smooth and light.   Stir in apples and raisins.

4. Stir flour mixture into the fruit mixture, mixing well; turn into greased bowl.

5. Cover surface of pudding with double thickness of waxed paper. Cover top of bowl completely with foil; tie edge securely with twine.

6. Place bowl on trivet in large kettle.   Pour boiling water around bowl to come halfway up side.

7. Cover kettle; bring to boiling.   Reduce heat; boil gently 2 hours.

8. Remove bowl to wire rack; let stand 5 minutes.

9. With spatula, gently loosen edge of pudding from side of bowl. Invert on serving dish.   Serve warm, with cream.

Makes 6 to 8 servings.

Chilled Raspberry Pudding

1 package (10 ounces) frozen   ¼ cup quick-cooking tapioca
   raspberries, thawed and
   undrained   ½ cup heavy cream
½ cup granulated sugar   2 tablespoons confectioners'
1 tablespoon grated lemon peel   sugar
1 cup port

1. In medium-size saucepan, combine raspberries, granulated sugar, lemon peel, port, and 1 cup water.

2. Bring mixture to boiling, stirring.   Reduce heat; simmer, covered, 10 minutes.

3. Stir in tapioca; bring back to boiling.   Reduce heat; cook, stirring constantly, until mixture becomes thickened and translucent.

4. Let cool.   Turn into 4 dessert dishes.   Refrigerate until very well chilled—about 2 hours.

5. Just before serving, whip cream with confectioners' sugar until stiff.   Spoon on pudding in mounds.

Makes 4 servings.

Cakes & Cookies

Baked goods, such as cakes and cookies, are usually eaten in Germany as a meal in themselves, accompanied only by coffee. They appear at the daily Kaffee between lunch and supper, or for late-night coffee drinking. The coffee table is set with fine dishes, flowers, and an array of exquisite baked delights. (A proper coffee party never has simply one cake or cookie offering.) There may be Honey-Nut Kuchen, Fresh-Apple Cake with Walnuts, a Chocolate-Hazelnut Torte, and a wide selection of cookies, like Almond Crescents, Pfeffernüsse, or Springerle. Certain pastries are associated with special holidays. Berliner Pfannkuchen are prepared on Shrove Tuesday, and Lebkuchen are always made at Christmastime. Of course, since these sweets are so good, you will not want to wait until the holidays roll around to try them.

Perhaps the crown of German baking is strudel. It can be difficult to prepare, but the delicate many-layered crispness of strudel is worth the effort. The trick in baking it is to stretch the dough with one's fists without tearing it. The recipe on page 74 will produce a strudel dough as thin and fine as tissue.

CAKES

Applecake

3 tablespoons butter or margarine, softened

⅓ cup light-brown sugar, firmly packed

2 cups sifted all-purpose flour
1⅓ cups granulated sugar
4 teaspoons baking powder
1 teaspoon salt
2 eggs, well beaten

1 cup milk
2 cups pared, sliced tart
    cooking apples
1 teaspoon cinnamon

1. Preheat oven to 350°F. Lightly grease 11- by 7- by 1½-inch baking pan.

2. In small bowl, with fork, mix butter and brown sugar well: set aside.

3. Sift flour, granulated sugar, baking powder, and salt into large bowl.

4. Combine eggs with milk; pour into dry ingredients. With rotary beater or electric mixer, beat about 1 minute, or until well combined. Turn into baking pan.

5. Place apples on batter (during baking, they are distributed through cake).

6. Sprinkle with ½ teaspoon cinnamon; top with butter-sugar mixture; sprinkle with rest of cinnamon; bake 35 to 40 minutes. Partially cool on wire rack. Serve warm.

Makes 8 servings.

Fresh-Apple Cake with Walnuts

2 cups unsifted all-purpose
    flour
2 cups sugar
2 teaspoons baking soda
1 teaspoon cinnamon
½ teaspoon nutmeg
½ teaspoon salt

4 cups pared, finely diced
    apples (about 1½ pounds)
½ cup chopped walnuts
½ cup butter or margarine,
    softened
2 eggs

1. Preheat oven to 325°F. Grease a 13- by 9- by 2-inch baking pan.

2. Into large bowl, sift flour with sugar, baking soda, cinnamon, nutmeg, salt.

3. Add apples, nuts, butter, eggs. Beat until just combined—it will be thick. Turn into prepared pan.

4. Bake 1 hour, or until top springs back when lightly pressed with fingertip. Cool in pan on wire rack.

5. Serve warm, cut into squares. Top with whipped cream or ice cream, if desired.

Makes 10 to 12 servings.

Apfelkuchen

1 egg	**Topping**
¼ cup milk	¼ cup granulated sugar
1 teaspoon vanilla extract	½ teaspoon cinnamon
¼ cup granulated sugar	¼ cup butter or margarine,
2 cups packaged biscuit mix	melted
¼ cup butter or margarine,	
softened	½ cup heavy cream
3 cups thinly sliced pared	2 tablespoons confectioners'
apples	sugar

1. Preheat oven to 375°F. Lightly butter a 9-inch springform pan or a 9- by 1½-inch layer-cake pan.

2. In medium-size bowl, with fork, beat egg with milk and vanilla until well mixed. Add ¼ cup granulated sugar, the biscuit mix, and ¼ cup softened butter; beat with fork until smooth—about 1 minute.

3. Spread batter evenly in prepared pan. On surface of batter, arrange apples, overlapping closely, around edge; then fill in center.

4. Make Topping: In small bowl, toss granulated sugar with cinnamon and melted butter; spoon over apple slices.

5. Bake 30 minutes, or until apples are tender. Remove to wire rack. Let cool 15 minutes, then remove side of springform pan. (If baking kuchen in layer-cake pan, it can be served right from pan.)

6. Meanwhile, in small bowl, whip cream just until stiff; add confectioners' sugar. Refrigerate until serving.

7. Serve kuchen in wedges while still warm, with chilled whipped cream.

Makes 8 servings.

Note: If kuchen is cut while it is too hot, it will be crumbly.

Black-Forest Cake

Cake	
½ cup butter or margarine	**Syrup**
6 eggs	½ cup granulated sugar
1 cup granulated sugar	¼ cup kirsch or brandy
½ cup sifted all-purpose flour	
⅓ cup sifted unsweetened dark	**Frosting**
cocoa	2 cups heavy cream
1 teaspoon vanilla extract	¼ cup unsifted confectioners'
	sugar
	2 tablespoons kirsch or brandy
	Shaved chocolate

1. Make Cake: Preheat oven to 350°F. Lightly grease and flour 2 (9-inch) layer-cake pans.

2. Melt butter over very low heat; set aside.

3. Warm large bowl of electric mixer over pan of boiling water (water should not touch bottom of bowl).

4. In warm bowl, beat eggs slightly with 1 cup sugar. Let stand over water, stirring occasionally, until eggs are lukewarm—5 to 10 minutes.

5. Meanwhile, sift flour with cocoa; set aside.

6. When eggs seem lukewarm to the touch, beat, at high speed, 10 to 15 minutes, until mixture has tripled in bulk and is as thick as whipped cream.

7. With wire whip or rubber scraper, gently fold flour mixture into egg mixture until thoroughly combined.

8. Fold in melted butter and vanilla, mixing well.

9. Turn batter into prepared pans; bake 25 to 30 minutes, or until surface springs back when gently pressed with fingertip.

10. Let cake layers cool in pans on wire racks several minutes; then loosen edges, and turn out on wire racks.

11. Meanwhile, make Syrup: In small saucepan, combine ½ cup sugar with 2 tablespoons water. Bring to boiling; reduce heat, and boil gently until mixture is thick and syrupy—about 5 minutes.

12. Stir in ¼ cup kirsch or brandy. Sprinkle syrup evenly over warm cake layers.

13. Make Frosting: In small bowl of electric mixer, combine cream with confectioners' sugar; refrigerate, along with beater, 1 hour.

14. Beat just until stiff; gradually beat in 2 tablespoons kirsch or brandy.

15. On serving plate, put cake layers together with one-third frosting. Use rest to frost top and side.

16. Sprinkle top with chocolate; refrigerate 1 hour before serving. Makes 10 to 12 servings.

Marble Cheesecake

Cookie Crust
¾ cup sugar
½ cup soft shortening
1¼ cups plus 2 tablespoons cake flour
1 tablespoon beaten egg
⅛ teaspoon salt
⅛ teaspoon grated lemon peel
2 tablespoons packaged dry bread crumbs

Cheese Filling
3½ packages (8-ounce size) cream cheese
1 container (8 ounces) skim-milk cottage cheese, well drained
1¼ cups sugar
3 eggs
2 tablespoons heavy cream
2 teaspoons vanilla extract
3 squares semisweet chocolate, melted

1½ Vandens
Saukstukue

1. Make Cookie Crust: Preheat oven to 350°F.

2. In large bowl, combine ¾ cup sugar, the shortening, cake flour, egg, 1½ teaspoons water, the salt, lemon peel. With electric mixer, beat at medium speed until well combined and dough leaves side of bowl.

3. Form dough into a ball. Fit onto bottom of a 9-inch springform pan, rolling lightly with rolling pin to make a smooth surface. Trim pastry ⅛ inch from edge all around. Prick with fork to prevent shrinkage.

4. Bake 10 minutes. Remove from oven; cool on wire rack 15 minutes. Then lightly grease inside of side of springform pan. Sprinkle lightly with bread crumbs, and attach side to bottom of pan with cookie crust. Retrim crust, if necessary.

5. Meanwhile, make Cheese Filling: Increase oven temperature to 400°F.

6. In large bowl, with electric mixer, combine cream cheese, cottage cheese, and sugar. Beat at medium speed until mixture is smooth and creamy.

7. Beat in eggs, one at a time, beating well after each addition. Beat in cream and vanilla.

8. Pour half of batter into prepared springform pan. Drizzle 2 tablespoons melted chocolate over batter. With finger, lightly swirl chocolate over surface.

9. Repeat with rest of batter and chocolate.

10. Bake 15 minutes. Remove to wire rack. Let cake cool in pan 45 minutes. Heat oven to 350°F.

11. Bake cake 25 minutes longer. Let cool completely on wire rack in pan. Refrigerate several hours or overnight, if possible, before serving.

12. Gently remove side of springform pan before serving.

Makes 8 to 10 servings.

Chocolate-Hazelnut Torte

Torte Layers
9 eggs
1¼ cups granulated sugar
⅓ cup golden rum
½ pound shelled hazelnuts,
    ground (about 2½ cups)

Filling
1½ cups confectioners' sugar
1¼ cups sweet butter, softened
¼ cup golden rum
3 egg yolks
4 squares unsweetened
    chocolate, melted and cooled

Frosting

2 squares unsweetened
   chocolate
2 tablespoons butter or
   margarine
1 cup confectioners' sugar
½ teaspoon vanilla extract

10 whole shelled hazelnuts
1 cup coarsely chopped
   hazelnuts

1. Make Torte Layers: Separate 9 eggs, putting whites in large bowl of electric mixer and yolks in small bowl. Let whites warm to room temperature.

2. Preheat oven to 350°F. Line bottoms of 3 (9-inch) layer-cake pans with waxed paper.

3. With mixer at high speed, beat egg whites until soft peaks form. Gradually beat in 1 cup granulated sugar; continue beating until stiff peaks form.

4. With same beaters, beat egg yolks with remaining granulated sugar until thick and lemon-colored—about 3 minutes. Stir in ⅓ cup rum and the ground hazelnuts until well blended.

5. With wire whip or rubber scraper, fold nut mixture into egg whites. Turn into prepared layer-cake pans.

6. Bake 30 minutes, or until surface springs back when lightly pressed with fingertip. Let cool completely in pans on wire rack. (Centers of layers may sink slightly.)

7. Make Filling: In medium-size bowl, combine 1½ cups confectioners' sugar, the sweet butter, rum, and egg yolks; beat with electric mixer until well blended. Add melted chocolate; beat well.

8. Make Frosting: In small bowl, melt chocolate and butter, over hot water. Remove from heat; blend in sugar, 2 tablespoons hot water, and vanilla until well blended and smooth.

9. With small spatula, gently loosen cooled torte layers from pans; carefully remove, and peel off wax paper.

10. Put layers together, using about ½ cup filling between layers. Set aside ½ cup filling for decoration, and spread remaining filling on side of torte. Spread top with frosting.

11. With reserved filling in pastry bag with number-30 star tip, pipe rosettes around top edge of torte. Place whole hazelnuts on top of torte, and pipe a border of filling around each. Press chopped hazelnuts against sides. Refrigerate 1 hour, or until firm enough to cut. (If refrigerated longer than an hour, let stand at room temperature to warm slightly.)

Makes 16 servings.

Honey-Nut Kuchen

¾ cup warm water (105° to
   115°F.)
2 packages active dry yeast
½ cup sugar
1 teaspoon salt
½ cup butter or margarine,
   softened
3 eggs
4¼ cups unsifted all-purpose
   flour
¼ teaspoon nutmeg

Honey Glaze
2 tablespoons sugar
¼ cup unsifted all-purpose flour
⅓ cup honey
¼ cup orange marmalade
¼ cup butter or margarine,
   softened

½ cup pecan halves

1. Sprinkle yeast over warm water in large bowl, stirring until yeast is dissolved. Add ½ cup sugar and the salt, stirring until dissolved.

2. Add ½ cup butter, the eggs, 3 cups flour, and the nutmeg. Beat vigorously with wooden spoon, or with electric mixer at medium speed, until smooth—about 2 minutes.

3. Gradually add remaining 1¼ cups flour, mixing with a wooden spoon, then with hands until dough is smooth and stiff enough to leave side of bowl.

4. Turn out dough onto lightly floured surface. Knead until smooth and blisters appear on surface—about 5 minutes.

5. Place in lightly greased large bowl; turn to bring greased side up. Cover with damp towel; let rise in warm place (85°F.), free from drafts, until double in bulk—1 to 1½ hours.

6. Butter generously the bottom and side of a 10½-inch skillet with a heat-resistant handle. (Wrap foil around handle to protect it, if necessary.

7. Turn out dough onto a lightly floured pastry cloth. With palms of hands, roll dough into a rope 36 inches long. Into prepared skillet, beginning at outside edge, turn dough into a coil, twisting dough at same time.

8. Cover with damp towel; let rise in warm place until double in bulk (dough should rise to top of skillet)—50 to 60 minutes.

9. Meanwhile, make Honey Glaze: In small bowl, combine sugar and flour; mix well. Add rest of ingredients, mixing until well combined.

10. Preheat oven to 350°F.

11. Bake 20 minutes. Then spoon half of Honey Glaze over top of dough, but not on outer edge; bake 10 minutes. Spoon rest of glaze over top. Arrange pecans on top—in grooves. Bake 5 minutes longer, or until kuchen is a rich golden brown.

12. Let cool in pan on wire rack 15 minutes. Remove from pan. Serve at once, or let cool completely.

13. To store, wrap in foil; store in freezer several weeks.

14. To serve frozen kuchen, preheat oven to 400°F. Heat foil-wrapped frozen kuchen (loosen foil slightly) 30 to 35 minutes, or just until heated through.

Makes 1 large kuchen.

Kugelhopf

½ cup light or dark raisins
½ cup currants
1 can (4½ ounces) blanched almonds, finely chopped
1 tablespoon grated lemon peel
1 tablespoon cognac or brandy
1 cup milk
1 cup granulated sugar
½ cup warm water (105° to 115°F.)
1 package active dry yeast

5 cups unsifted all-purpose flour
14 to 16 whole blanched almonds
1 cup butter or margarine, softened
1 teaspoon salt
6 eggs
¼ cup butter or margarine, melted

Confectioners' sugar

1. In medium-size bowl, combine raisins, currants, chopped almonds (reserve ¼ cup for later use), lemon peel, and cognac; toss lightly to mix well. Set aside.

2. In small saucepan, heat milk until bubbles form around edge of pan; remove from heat. Stir in ¼ cup granulated sugar; let cool to lukewarm.

3. Sprinkle yeast over warm water in large bowl; stir until dissolved. Stir in lukewarm milk mixture and 3 cups flour; with wooden spoon, beat until smooth—about 2 minutes.

4. Cover bowl with damp towel; let rise in warm place (85°F.), free from drafts, until double in bulk—about 1 hour. Batter will be light and spongy.

5. Meanwhile, butter generously a 4-quart Turk's-head tube mold, 10½ inches in diameter. Sprinkle inside of mold evenly with reserved chopped almonds. Place a whole almond in each indentation in the bottom of the mold.

6. In large bowl, with electric mixer at medium speed, beat softened butter with remaining granulated sugar and the salt until light and fluffy. Beat in eggs, one at a time, beating until smooth.

7. At low speed, beat in 1 cup flour and the risen batter until smooth and well blended.

8. With wooden spoon, stir in the remaining flour and the fruit-nut mixture, beating until well combined.

9. Pour batter into prepared mold. Cover with damp towel; let rise in warm place (85°F.), free from drafts, 1 hour, or until batter rises almost to top of pan.

10. Meanwhile, preheat oven to 350°F.

11. Bake Kugelhopf 50 to 60 minutes, or until a cake tester inserted near the center comes out clean. Let cool in pan on wire rack about 20 minutes.

12. Run spatula around sides of pan to loosen; turn out on wire rack. Brush with melted butter. Let cool completely.

13. To store, wrap in waxed paper, then in foil. Store in a cool, dry place or in the refrigerator if storing for a week or two. Store in freezer if keeping longer.

14. To serve, let warm to room temperature. Sprinkle lightly with confectioners' sugar. Slice thinly.

Makes 1 large Kugelhopf.

Mohn Cake

Pastry
1 stick (4 ounces) butter or margarine
1 package (13¾ ounces) hot-roll mix
¾ cup warm water (105° to 115°F.)
3 tablespoons sugar
1 egg, slightly beaten

Poppy-Seed Filling
1½ cups poppy seed
1 egg, slightly beaten
¼ cup fresh white-bread crumbs

⅔ cup honey
1 tablespoon lemon juice
¼ cup roasted slivered almonds
¼ cup chopped light or dark raisins
2 tablespoons butter or margarine, melted

Topping
⅓ cup honey
2 tablespoons lemon juice
½ cup roasted slivered almonds

1. Make Pastry: Cut butter lengthwise into quarters to form 4 strips. Refrigerate, wrapped in foil, until well chilled—about 1 hour.

2. In large, warm bowl, mix yeast from the hot-roll mix with warm water. Stir to dissolve yeast.

3. Add sugar and egg, then rest of hot-roll mix. Beat, with wooden spoon, until well mixed.

4. Turn out dough onto lightly floured surface. Knead, with hands, 5 to 8 minutes, or until smooth and elastic.

5. Roll dough to form a 12- by 9-inch rectangle. Arrange strips of chilled butter in single layer over half of dough, leaving a ½-inch border on 3 sides. Fold other half of dough over butter; with fingers, pinch edges together to form a seal.

6. With folded side of pastry at the left, roll out to form a 14- by 7-inch rectangle. Fold pastry into thirds. Repeat rolling and folding twice. Wrap in foil; refrigerate 30 minutes.

7. Lightly grease an 11- by 4½- by 2¾-inch loaf pan.

8. Meanwhile, make Poppy-Seed Filling: Grind poppy seed very fine in electric blender at high speed, or grind in mortar with pestle. Combine ground poppy seed with egg, bread crumbs, honey, lemon juice, almonds, and raisins; mix well.

9. Roll out chilled pastry to form an 11- by 14-inch rectangle. Spread filling lengthwise over pastry to cover lower two thirds. Fold uncovered third of pastry over filling, to cover it halfway, forming a pastry layer. Then fold bottom portion, spread with filling, over this pastry layer.

10. Place in prepared pan. Make cuts crosswise in surface of pastry at ½-inch intervals. Brush with melted butter.

11. Let stand at room temperature, covered with foil, 1 to 1½ hours, or until pastry comes halfway up side of pan.

12. Preheat oven to 375°F. Make Topping: Combine honey and lemon juice; heat gently. Use half to brush top of pastry. Sprinkle with almonds.

13. Bake 40 to 50 minutes, or until golden brown. Let cool in pan on wire rack until almost cold—about ¾ hour.

14. Loosen edges with sharp knife; turn out. Brush top again with the remaining honey mixture. Serve slightly warm.

Makes 10 to 12 servings.

Crusty Sesame Loaf

1 cup milk	1 package active dry yeast
2 tablespoons sugar	6 cups sifted all-purpose flour
2 teaspoons salt	1 egg white, slightly beaten
2 tablespoons butter or margarine	2 tablespoons sesame seed
1 cup warm water (105° to 115°F.)	

1. In small saucepan, heat milk just until bubbles form around edge of pan; remove from heat.

2. Add sugar, salt, and butter, stirring until butter is melted. Let cool to lukewarm.

3. Sprinkle yeast over water in large bowl, stirring until dissolved.

4. Stir in milk mixture. Add 3 cups flour; beat, with wooden spoon, until smooth—about 2 minutes.

5. Gradually add remaining flour; mix in last of it with hand until dough leaves side of bowl.

6. Turn dough onto lightly floured board. Knead until smooth and elastic—about 10 minutes.

7. Place in lightly greased large bowl; turn dough over to bring up greased side. Cover with damp towel; let rise in warm place (85°F.), free from drafts, until double in bulk—about 1 hour.

8. Grease a large cookie sheet.

9. Punch down dough; turn onto lightly floured pastry cloth. Divide in half. With palms, roll each into a 12-inch loaf, tapering ends.

10. Place, 4 inches apart, on prepared cookie sheet. With scissors, make 5 diagonal slashes across each loaf. Cover with towel; let rise in warm place (85°F.), free from drafts, until double in bulk—about 45 minutes.

11. Meanwhile, preheat oven to 400°F. Brush tops of loaves with egg white; bake 40 minutes. Brush again with egg white; sprinkle with sesame seed; bake 10 minutes. Remove loaves to wire rack; cool.

Makes 2 loaves.

Stollen

¾ cup milk	1 jar (8 ounces) diced mixed candied peel
½ cup granulated sugar	
½ teaspoon salt	½ cup finely chopped blanched almonds
1 package active dry yeast	
¼ cup warm water (105° to 115°F.)	1 cup butter or margarine, softened
5 cups unsifted all-purpose flour	½ teaspoon nutmeg or mace
1 cup dark raisins	2 eggs
1 tablespoon grated lemon peel	¼ cup butter or margarine, melted
1 jar (4 ounces) candied red cherries, coarsely chopped	Confectioners' sugar

1. In small saucepan, heat milk just until bubbles form around edge of pan; remove from heat. Add granulated sugar and salt, stirring until dissolved. Let cool to lukewarm (a drop on wrist won't feel warm).

2. In large bowl that has been rinsed in hot water, sprinkle yeast over warm water; stir until dissolved.

3. Stir in milk mixture and 2 cups flour; beat with wooden spoon until smooth—at least 2 minutes.

4. Cover bowl with damp towel; let rise in warm place (85°F.), free from drafts, until double in bulk—1½ hours.   Grease 2 cookie sheets.

5. Add the raisins, lemon peel, candied fruit, almonds, softened butter, nutmeg, eggs, and remaining flour to risen dough in bowl. Mix with wooden spoon until blended. Turn out onto lightly floured surface; knead until fruit and nuts are well distributed—about 5 minutes.

6. Divide dough in half; shape each half into a ball. Roll or pat one ball into an oval 10 inches long and 6 inches across at widest part. Brush with 1 tablespoon melted butter.

7. Fold dough in half lengthwise. Place on prepared cookie sheet. Press folded edge lightly, to crease; then curve into crescent shape.   Repeat with other ball of dough.

8. Cover Stollen with damp towels; let rise in warm place (85°F.), free from drafts, until double in bulk—1½ to 2 hours.

9. Preheat oven to 375°F.

10. Bake 25 to 30 minutes, or until nicely browned. Brush tops of Stollen with remaining melted butter.

11. Remove to wire racks; cool.

12. To store, wrap in plastic wrap, then in foil.   Store in refrigerator or freezer several weeks.

13. To serve, let warm to room temperature. Just before serving, sprinkle with confectioners' sugar.

Makes 2 Stollen.

Streusel-Layered Coffeecake

Streusel Mixture

½ cup light-brown sugar, firmly
   packed
2 tablespoons butter or
   margarine, softened
2 tablespoons all-purpose flour
1 teaspoon cinnamon
½ cup coarsely chopped
   walnuts (optional)

Batter

1½ cups sifted all-purpose flour
2½ teaspoons baking powder
½ teaspoon salt
1 egg
¾ cup granulated sugar
⅓ cup butter or margarine,
   melted
½ cup milk
1 teaspoon vanilla extract

1. Preheat oven to 375°F.   Grease an 8- by 8- by 2-inch baking pan or a 9- by 1½-inch round layer-cake pan.

2. Make Streusel Mixture: In small bowl, combine brown sugar, 2 tablespoons softened butter, 2 tablespoons flour, the cinnamon, and nuts; mix with fork until crumbly.   Set aside.

3. Make Batter: Sift flour with baking powder and salt.   Set aside.

4. In medium-size bowl, with rotary beater, beat egg until frothy.

Beat in sugar and butter until well combined. Add milk and vanilla. With wooden spoon, stir in flour mixture until well combined.

5. Turn half of batter into prepared pan. Sprinkle evenly with half of streusel mixture. Repeat with remaining batter and streusel mixture.

6. Bake 25 to 30 minutes, or until cake tester inserted in center comes out clean. Cool slightly in pan on wire rack. Serve warm.

Makes 9 servings.

Blueberry Streusel Coffeecake

Streusel Topping
½ cup graham-cracker crumbs
¼ cup butter or margarine, softened
2 tablespoons sugar
½ teaspoon cinnamon

Coffeecake
2 cups sifted all-purpose flour
3 teaspoons baking powder
1 teaspoon salt
¼ cup sugar
¼ cup butter or margarine, softened
½ cup milk
1 egg
1½ cups fresh or thawed and drained frozen blueberries
Butter or margarine

1. Preheat oven to 400°F. Lightly grease and flour a 9- by 1½-inch round layer-cake pan. Set aside.

2. Make Streusel Topping: In a small bowl, combine graham-cracker crumbs, butter, sugar, and cinnamon. Toss lightly, with a fork, until the mixture is crumbly. Set aside.

3. Make Coffeecake: Into medium-size bowl, sift flour with baking powder, salt, and sugar. With a pastry blender, or 2 knives used scissor fashion, cut the butter into dry ingredients until mixture is consistency of coarse cornmeal.

4. Make a well in center of flour mixture. Pour in milk, all at once; then add the egg. Stir quickly, with a fork, just until all the ingredients are moistened and combined.

5. Spread batter evenly in prepared layer-cake pan. Arrange blueberries over surface of batter, leaving a 1-inch margin around edge of the pan.

6. Sprinkle topping evenly over blueberries.

7. Bake 30 minutes, or until top is nicely browned. Place the pan on a wire rack, and let the coffeecake cool slightly while still in the pan.

8. Serve while warm, cut into wedges, with butter or margarine.

Makes 9 or 10 servings.

Strudel Dough

5 tablespoons salad oil
2⅔ cups sifted all-purpose flour
¼ teaspoon salt
1 egg, slightly beaten
½ cup butter or margarine, melted

1. In 1-cup measure, combine ¾ cup warm water with 2 tablespoons salad oil.

2. Sift flour with salt onto wooden board.

3. Make well in center of flour mixture. Add egg to part of mixture, mixing well with hand. Gradually add oil mixture, mixing until all flour has been moistened. Dough will be sticky and smooth.

4. With hand, vigorously stretch dough up from board; then slap it down. Repeat 100 times, or until dough is no longer sticky. (Touch lightly with clean finger to test.)

5. Scrape up dough from board with metal spatula; shape into a ball. Brush surface with 1 tablespoon salad oil.

6. Rinse large bowl with hot water; dry. Invert over dough; let dough rest 30 minutes.

7. Meanwhile, prepare desired filling.

8. Spread clean cloth or sheet on kitchen table or card table. Sprinkle entire surface generously with flour; rub evenly into cloth.

9. Place dough in center of table. Starting from center, roll out dough to a 24-inch square, occasionally lifting dough to prevent its sticking to cloth.

10. Brush entire surface of dough with 2 tablespoons salad oil. Place backs of hands (remove any rings) under dough. Stretch dough gently, from center to outer edge, until it is as thin as tissue paper.

11. Trim uneven edges with scissors to form a 40- by 30-inch rectangle. Let stand 5 minutes to dry out.

12. Brush entire surface with melted butter. Then fill, roll, and bake as directed in recipes for Golden Apple Strudel (see below) and Fresh-Cherry Strudel (see p. 76).

Golden Apple Strudel

1 recipe Strudel Dough (see p. 74)

Apple Filling
6 cups (about 2 pounds) apples, pared, cored, and thinly sliced
½ cup granulated sugar
2 teaspoons grated lemon peel
1 cup packaged dry bread crumbs

½ cup finely chopped blanched almonds
½ teaspoon nutmeg
¼ cup butter or margarine, melted

1½ tablespoons butter or margarine, melted

Confectioners' sugar

1. Make Strudel Dough as recipe directs.

2. Meanwhile, make Apple Filling: In medium-size bowl, combine apples, granulated sugar, lemon peel, bread crumbs, almonds, nutmeg, and ¼ cup butter; toss lightly to combine.

3. Preheat oven to 375°F.   Grease a large cookie sheet.

4. Spoon filling crosswise over one end of dough.   Make a strip about 8 inches wide.

5. From filling side, roll up dough loosely, jelly-roll fashion, using cloth to roll it along.

6. Roll strudel onto prepared cookie sheet, turn seam side down. Bend strudel into horseshoe shape; tuck in ends to seal.   Brush entire surface with 1 tablespoon melted butter.

7. Bake 40 minutes, or until golden brown, brushing occasionally with rest of butter.

8. Remove to wire rack; cool.   Sprinkle with confectioners' sugar. Serve warm or cold, cut into slices.

Makes 12 servings.

Fresh-Cherry Strudel

1   recipe Strudel Dough (see p. 74)

Cherry Filling
½ cup granulated sugar
2   teaspoons grated lemon peel
1   cup packaged dry bread crumbs
½ teaspoon cinnamon
1   cup finely chopped walnuts

½ teaspoon almond extract
¼ cup butter or margarine, melted
4   cups fresh pitted Bing cherries, coarsely chopped

1½ tablespoons butter or margarine, melted

Confectioners' sugar

1. Make Strudel Dough as recipe directs.

2. Meanwhile, make Cherry Filling: In small bowl, combine granulated sugar, lemon peel, bread crumbs, cinnamon, walnuts, almond extract, and ¼ cup butter; toss lightly.

3. Preheat oven to 375°F.   Grease a large cookie sheet.

4. Sprinkle half of crumb mixture crosswise over one-fourth of dough. Spoon cherries evenly over mixture; top with rest of crumbs.

5. From filling side, roll up dough loosely, jelly-roll fashion, using cloth to roll it along.

6. Roll strudel onto prepared cookie sheet; turn seam side down.

Bend into a horseshoe shape; tuck in ends to seal.   Brush entire surface with 1 tablespoon melted butter.

7. Bake 40 minutes, or until golden brown, brushing occasionally with rest of butter.

8. Remove to wire rack; cool.   Sprinkle with confectioners' sugar. Serve warm or cold, cut into slices.

Makes 12 servings.

Warm Cream-Cheese Strudel

1 package (4 leaves) strudel leaves	2 teaspoons grated lemon peel
	⅓ cup melted butter or margarine
Cream-Cheese Filling	⅓ cup packaged dry bread crumbs
4 packages (3-ounce size) cream cheese, softened	
½ cup granulated sugar	
3 egg yolks	Confectioners' sugar
½ cup light raisins	

1. Let strudel leaves stand at room temperature overnight.

2. Next day, preheat oven to 375°F.   Grease a cookie sheet.

3. Prepare Cream-Cheese Filling: In small bowl of electric mixer, combine cream cheese, sugar, and egg yolks; beat at medium speed until well blended and smooth.   Stir in raisins and lemon peel.   Refrigerate.

4. Place a damp cloth (larger than 23- by 17-inch strudel leaves) on work surface.   Remove 2 leaves from box of strudel leaves.   Unfold leaves on damp cloth.   Quickly brush 1 leaf with melted butter; then sprinkle with about 1 tablespoon bread crumbs.   Top with second leaf; quickly brush with butter, and sprinkle with crumbs.

5. Remove remaining 2 leaves from box; brush each with butter, and sprinkle with crumbs.   Place on first 2 leaves to make 4 layers.   Spread filling over half of top leaf, starting from one short end.   Then, from same end, roll up pastry loosely, jelly-roll fashion, using cloth to roll and guide it.

6. Roll strudel onto prepared cookie sheet, placing seam side down. Brush with butter.

7. Bake 50 to 55 minutes, or until deep golden brown.   Brush with any remaining butter.

8. Remove to wire rack.   Let cool 30 minutes; then sprinkle with

confectioners' sugar.   Serve warm, cut into thick slices.
  Makes 6 servings.

Berliner Pfannkuchen

½ cup milk
⅓ cup sugar
1 teaspoon salt
⅓ cup butter or margarine
2 packages active dry yeast
½ cup warm water (105° to
    115°F.)
3 egg yolks
3¾ cups sifted all-purpose
    flour

Raspberry or strawberry jam
    or jelly
Egg white

Salad oil for deep-frying

Granulated sugar

  1. Heat milk in small saucepan until bubbles form around edge of pan; remove from heat.   Add ⅓ cup sugar, the salt, and butter; stir until butter is melted.   Let cool to lukewarm.
  2. In large bowl, sprinkle yeast over warm water.   Stir until dissolved.
  3. Add milk mixture, egg yolks, and 2 cups flour.   With electric mixer at medium speed, beat until smooth—about 2 minutes.
  4. With wooden spoon, beat in remaining flour; beat until smooth.
  5. Cover with foil; let rise in warm place (85°F.), free from drafts, until double in bulk—about 1 hour.
  6. Punch down dough.   Turn out onto lightly floured surface; turn over to coat with flour.   Knead 10 times, or until dough is smooth.   Divide in half.
  7. Roll out half of dough to ¼-inch thickness.   Cut into 14 (3-inch) rounds.   Place 1 teaspoon jam in center of half of rounds; brush edge with egg white.   Top with plain rounds, and press together firmly to seal.   Arrange on floured cookie sheet.   Repeat with rest of dough.
  8. Cover with damp towel; let rise until double in bulk—about 45 minutes.
  9. Meanwhile, in deep-fat fryer, electric skillet, or heavy skillet, slowly heat salad oil (2 inches deep) to 375°F. on deep-frying thermometer.
  10. Gently drop doughnuts, 3 or 4 at a time, into hot oil.   Fry, turning as they rise to surface, until golden brown—about 4 minutes in all. (Break one open to test for doneness.   Fry others longer if necessary.)
  11. Remove with slotted utensil.   Drain on paper towels.   While still warm, dust with sugar.
  Makes 14.

COOKIES

Almond Crescents

Almond Filling
1 can (8 ounces) almond paste
½ cup butter or margarine,
   softened
1 teaspoon grated lemon peel
2 teaspoons lemon juice

2 packages (8-ounce size)
   refrigerator crescent rolls

Icing
1 cup confectioners' sugar
2 tablespoons butter or
   margarine
1 tablespoon milk

1. Make Almond Filling: Combine almond paste with ½ cup butter, the lemon peel, and lemon juice; mix well.

2. Preheat oven to 375°F.

3. Unroll crescent-roll dough from both packages. Cut along perforations to make 16 pieces of dough.

4. Spread each with 1 tablespoon filling; roll up as package label directs.

5. Place, 2 inches apart, on an ungreased cookie sheet; bake 10 to 15 minutes, or until golden.

6. Meanwhile, make Icing: In small bowl, combine sugar, 2 tablespoons butter, and the milk; mix until smooth.

7. Remove crescents to wire rack. Spread tops with icing. Serve warm.

Makes 16 crescents.

Chocolate-Butter Cream Continentals

1 cup butter or margarine
4 egg whites
1 cup sugar
4 egg yolks
2 cups sifted all-purpose flour
6 drops red food coloring
1½ cups dairy sour cream

1 can (4½ ounces) toasted
   almonds, finely chopped
½ cup apricot preserves
½ cup red-raspberry jam

Chocolate-Butter Cream (see
   p. 80)

1. Preheat oven to 350°F. Grease, then flour bottoms of two 9- by 9- by 2-inch baking pans. In large bowl, let butter stand at room temperature until softened.

2. In medium-size bowl, with electric mixer, beat egg whites until soft peaks form when beater is slowly raised. Set aside.

3. With same beater, at high speed, beat butter with sugar and egg yolks until light and fluffy.

4. At low speed, beat in flour just until combined. Fold in egg whites.

5. With spatula, spread a scant ½ cup batter on bottom of each prepared pan to within ¼ inch of edge. Bake 10 minutes, or just until edges of cakes are golden brown. Carefully remove each layer to wire rack.

6. Wash and dry pans; grease and flour again. Spread each with batter and bake as in step 5.

7. Stir food coloring into remaining batter. Use to make 3 pink layers.

8. Mix sour cream with almonds.

9. Place 1 yellow layer, top side up, on cookie sheet. Spread with one-third of apricot preserves, then with ⅓ cup sour-cream mixture. Add pink layer. Spread with one-third of raspberry jam, then with ⅓ cup sour-cream mixture. Continue adding layers, alternating yellow and pink layers and preserves and jam. Leave top layer plain.

10. Set board or heavy, flat pan on top of cake to weigh it down. Refrigerate overnight.

11. Next day, trim edges of cake. Spread ½ cup Chocolate-Butter Cream over top of cake. Place remaining butter cream in pastry bag with tiny star decorating tip, and decorate cake.

12. Cut into 3- by 1-inch bars, and store, covered, in refrigerator. Makes 24.

Chocolate-Butter Cream

2 cups confectioners' sugar	½ teaspoon vanilla extract
¼ cup unsweetened cocoa	4 to 5 tablespoons heavy
¼ cup butter or margarine,	cream or undiluted
softened	evaporated milk

1. In medium-size bowl, combine sugar, cocoa, butter, vanilla, and 4 tablespoons cream.

2. With electric mixer at medium speed, beat until smooth and creamy. Add more cream if it seems too stiff. Use to decorate Chocolate-Butter Cream Continentals.

Makes 1⅓ cups.

Christmas Cookies

4 cups sifted all-purpose flour	1 teaspoon vanilla extract
1 teaspoon baking powder	
½ teaspoon salt	Decorating Frosting (see
1 teaspoon nutmeg	below)
¾ cup butter or margarine, softened	
1¼ cups granulated sugar	Colored sugar, colored dragées, nonpareils, chocolate pieces
2 eggs	

1. On sheet of waxed paper, sift flour with baking powder, salt, and nutmeg. Set aside.

2. In large bowl of electric mixer, at high speed, beat butter, granulated sugar, eggs, and vanilla until light and fluffy.

3. With wooden spoon, stir in half of flour mixture. Then add rest of flour mixture, mixing with hands if necessary.

4. Refrigerate dough, covered, several hours or overnight.

5. Preheat oven to 400°F. Divide dough into 4 parts; refrigerate until ready to roll out.

6. Between 2 sheets of waxed paper, on slightly dampened surface, roll out dough, one part at a time, ⅛ inch thick.

7. With floured, assorted cookie cutters, cut out cookies. Place, 2 inches apart, on ungreased cookie sheets.

8. Bake 8 minutes, or just until set and lightly brown around the edges. Remove to wire rack; cool completely.

9. Spread cookies evenly with Decorating Frosting. Decorate with colored sugar, dragées, nonpareils, and chocolate pieces. Let dry on wire rack about 1 hour.

10. Store in airtight cookie jar or tin, in a cool, dry place, several weeks.

Makes 3 to 4 dozen.

Decorating Frosting

2 egg whites	1¾ cups sifted confectioners' sugar
⅛ teaspoon cream of tartar	Food coloring

1. In medium-size bowl, with electric mixer at high speed, beat egg whites with cream of tartar until stiff peaks form when beater is slowly raised.

2. Gradually add the confectioners' sugar, beating until frosting is smooth and thin enough to spread. (If necessary, add 1 to 2 tablespoons water to thin it.)

3. Divide into 3 parts. Tint each with 1 or 2 drops of different food coloring.

4. Cover with a damp cloth until ready to spread on Christmas cookies.

Honey Cakes

3 cups unsifted all-purpose flour	2 tablespoons grated lemon peel
½ teaspoon baking soda	½ cup honey
½ teaspoon salt	1 cup light-brown sugar, firmly packed
1 teaspoon cinnamon	
½ teaspoon nutmeg	2 eggs
½ teaspoon ground ginger	
½ teaspoon ground cloves	2 cups sifted confectioners' sugar
1 jar (8 ounces) chopped candied orange peel	
1 jar (8 ounces) chopped candied lemon peel	Candied red cherries
½ cup ground unblanched almonds	Angelica

1. On sheet of waxed paper, sift flour with baking soda, salt, and spices. Set aside.

2. Toss candied peels with almonds and grated lemon peel to mix well. Set aside.

3. In small saucepan, warm honey; remove from heat.

4. In large bowl of electric mixer, at high speed, beat brown sugar and eggs until smooth and fluffy. Add honey; beat well. Add 1 cup flour mixture; beat, at low speed, just until smooth.

5. Using a wooden spoon, stir in rest of flour mixture until well combined. Then stir in peel-and-nut mixture.

6. Refrigerate dough, covered, overnight.

7. Next day, preheat oven to 375°F. Lightly grease several cookie sheets.

8. On lightly floured pastry cloth, roll out dough, one half at a time, ¼ inch thick. (Refrigerate remaining half until ready to roll out.)

9. Using floured, 2-inch cookie cutters, cut out cookies. Place, 2 inches apart, on prepared cookie sheets. Bake 10 to 12 minutes. Remove cookies to wire rack.

10. Make glaze: In small bowl, combine confectioners' sugar with 3 tablespoons water; stir until smooth.

11. Brush glaze on warm cookies. Decorate at once with bits of candied cherries and angelica. Let cool completely.

12. To store: Store in a glass jar or crock or cookie tin, tightly covered, in a cool, dry place for several weeks.   Store cookies with a piece of apple to keep them moist.

Makes about 7 dozen.

Lebkuchen Rounds

3 cups sifted all-purpose flour	¾ cup light-brown sugar, firmly
½ teaspoon baking soda	packed
½ teaspoon salt	1 egg
1 teaspoon ground allspice	1 tablespoon lemon juice
1 teaspoon nutmeg	2 teaspoons grated lemon peel
1 teaspoon cinnamon	
1 teaspoon ground cloves	2 cups sifted confectioners'
1 jar (4 ounces) citron,	sugar
finely chopped	
1 can (4 ounces) walnuts,	Candied red cherries (optional)
finely chopped	Angelica (optional)
1 cup honey	

1. Sift flour with baking soda, salt, and spices; set aside.   Toss citron with walnuts; set aside.

2. Warm honey in small saucepan.   Remove from heat.

3. In large bowl, using electric mixer at medium speed, beat brown sugar and egg until smooth and fluffy.

4. Add lemon juice and honey; beat well.   Beat in lemon peel and 1 cup flour mixture; beat until smooth.

5. Using wooden spoon, stir in rest of flour mixture until well combined.   Stir in citron-nut mixture.

6. Refrigerate dough, covered, overnight.

7. Next day, preheat oven to 375°F.   Lightly grease 2 cookie sheets.

8. On lightly floured surface, roll out dough, one half at a time, ¼ inch thick.   (Refrigerate remaining half until ready to roll out.)

9. Using floured 2-inch round cookie cutter, cut out cookies.   Place, 2 inches apart, on prepared cookie sheets; bake 15 minutes.   Remove to wire rack; cool slightly.

10. Meanwhile, make glaze: Combine confectioners' sugar with 3 tablespoons water; stir until smooth.

11. Brush glaze on warm cookies.   Decorate with candied cherry and angelica bits, if desired.   Let cookies cool completely.

12. Store, tightly covered, in a cool, dry place 2 to 3 weeks before using.   (To keep cookies moist, keep a slice of bread in container, changing bread from time to time to prevent molding.)

Makes 3 dozen.

Leckerli

¼ cup candied orange peel	4 cups sifted all-purpose flour
¼ cup candied lemon peel	Dash salt
1½ cups whole unblanched almonds	1 teaspoon baking soda
	1 teaspoon cinnamon
¾ cup honey	Dash ground cloves
1¼ cups granulated sugar	Dash nutmeg
1 tablespoon grated lemon peel	
¼ cup lemon juice	1 cup confectioners' sugar
1½ tablespoons kirsch or brandy	Candied red cherries

1. Put candied orange and lemon peel and almonds through fine blade of food grinder or grind in blender until very fine.

2. In medium-size saucepan, bring honey and granulated sugar just to boiling, stirring (do not boil). Add fresh lemon peel and lemon juice. Set aside to cool—10 minutes. Then add ground peel and almonds and the kirsch.

3. Sift flour with salt, baking soda, cinnamon, cloves, and nutmeg into a large bowl. Make well in center of flour mixture; pour in fruit-and-honey mixture. Work together, with a kneading motion, until well combined. Dough will be quite stiff.

4. Preheat oven to 350°F.

5. Divide dough into 4 parts. Refrigerate 3 parts until ready to use. Between 2 sheets of waxed paper, on slightly dampened surface, roll out one part to form a rectangle 6 by 8 inches, ¼ inch thick. Cut into 16 rectangles. Place, about 1 inch apart, on ungreased cookie sheets.

6. Bake about 10 minutes, or just until golden.

7. Repeat with rest of dough.

8. In small bowl, combine confectioners' sugar with 3 tablespoons water; stir to mix well. Brush over cookies while they are still warm. Decorate with bits of candied cherries.

9. Store in a tightly covered jar or plastic container, in a cool, dry place, several weeks.

Makes 64.

Linzer Torte

Packaged dry bread crumbs	1½ teaspoons baking powder
	¾ cup butter or margarine
Crust	1 egg
2⅔ cups sifted all-purpose flour	1 egg yolk
½ cup granulated sugar	

Almond Filling
1 cup butter or margarine
2 cups confectioners' sugar
2 cups ground almonds

4 eggs

1 jar (12 ounces) red-raspberry
   jam

1. Grease a 15- by 10- by 1-inch jelly-roll pan. Sprinkle bottom and sides with bread crumbs.

2. Make Crust: Sift flour, granulated sugar, and baking powder together into a bowl. With pastry blender, cut in ¾ cup butter until mixture resembles fine cornmeal. With a fork, beat in 1 egg and the egg yolk; knead with hands to make a smooth dough. Shape into a ball; divide in half.

3. Between 2 sheets of waxed paper, roll out half of dough to a 13- by 9-inch rectangle. Fit into prepared pan, from center to one end. Tuck in overhang to make edge even with top of pan. Repeat with other half of dough, fitting into other end of pan. Press edges of dough together in center. Refrigerate while making filling.

4. Preheat oven to 325°F.

5. Make Almond Filling: In medium-size bowl, with electric mixer, beat butter until creamy. Beat in sugar and almonds until thoroughly mixed. Beat in eggs, one at a time, beating well after each addition.

6. Sieve jam. Spread half over chilled crust. Top with almond filling.

7. Bake 55 to 60 minutes, or until top is golden and crust pulls away from sides of pan. Cool in pan on wire rack.

8. Spread remaining jam over top. To serve, cut into 2- by 1-inch strips.
Makes 75 strips.

Pecan Crescents

2 cups unsifted all-purpose
   flour
1 cup butter or margarine,
   softened
1 cup ground pecans or
   hazel nuts
½ cup unsifted confectioners'
   sugar
⅛ teaspoon salt

1 teaspoon vanilla extract
¼ teaspoon almond extract

Vanilla Sugar
1 (3-inch) strip vanilla bean,
   cut up
2 cups sifted confectioners'
   sugar

1. In large bowl, combine flour, butter, nuts, ½ cup sugar, salt, and extracts. Mix, with hands, until thoroughly combined. Refrigerate, covered, 1 hour.

2. Make Vanilla Sugar: In electric blender, combine cut-up vanilla

bean and ¼ cup confectioners' sugar; cover; blend at high speed about 8 seconds. Combine with remaining confectioners' sugar on a large sheet of foil.

3. Preheat oven to 375°F.

4. Shape cookies: Form dough into balls, using 1 tablespoon dough for each. Then, with palms of hands, form each ball into a roll 3 inches long.

5. Place, 2 inches apart, on ungreased cookie sheets. Curve each to make a crescent. Bake 12 to 15 minutes, or until set but not brown.

6. Let stand 1 minute before removing. With spatula, place hot cookies in vanilla sugar; turn gently to coat both sides. Cool completely.

7. Store in a tightly covered crock or cookie tin in a cool, dry place.

8. Just before serving, coat with additional vanilla sugar if desired. Makes about 3½ dozen.

Pfeffernüsse

Cookie Dough
2½ cups unsifted all-purpose flour
½ teaspoon ground cloves
½ teaspoon nutmeg
½ teaspoon cinnamon
¼ teaspoon ground ginger
¼ teaspoon black pepper
¼ teaspoon ground cardamom
¼ teaspoon baking soda

2 eggs
1 cup dark-brown sugar, firmly packed
⅓ cup finely chopped walnuts

Glaze
3 cups granulated sugar
Dash cream of tartar
2 egg whites

1. Make Cookie Dough: Sift flour with cloves, nutmeg, cinnamon, ginger, pepper, cardamom, and baking soda. Set aside.

2. In large bowl, with electric beater at high speed, beat 2 eggs and the brown sugar until light—about 5 minutes.

3. At low speed, beat in flour mixture and nuts until well combined. Dough will be sticky.

4. Preheat oven to 375°F. Lightly grease cookie sheets.

5. With wet hands, pinch off dough by tablespoonfuls. Roll into 1-inch balls.

6. Place on prepared cookie sheets. Bake 12 to 15 minutes. Remove to wire rack to cool.

7. Meanwhile, make Glaze: In large saucepan, combine sugar, cream of tartar, and 1 cup water. Bring to boiling over medium heat, stirring until sugar is dissolved. Boil, without stirring, 5 minutes, or until mixture forms a 2-inch thread when dropped from a spoon, or to 235°F. on candy thermometer.

8. Meanwhile, in medium-size bowl, with electric mixer at medium speed, beat egg whites until stiff peaks form when beater is raised. Pour syrup in continuous stream into egg whites, beating constantly. Beat until mixture thickens slightly.

9. Drop cookies, a few at a time, into glaze, with fork, turn to coat completely. Lift out, and place on wire rack to dry.

10. Store in tightly covered container about 1 week, to mellow. Makes about 3½ dozen.

Springerle

2 cups sifted all-purpose flour	1 teaspoon grated lemon peel
½ teaspoon baking powder	
¼ teaspoon salt	1½ tablespoons anise seed
2 eggs	
1 cup granulated sugar	Confectioners' sugar

1. On sheet of waxed paper, sift flour with baking powder and salt twice. Set aside.

2. In medium-size bowl, with electric mixer at high speed, beat eggs until thick and lemon-colored—about 5 minutes.

3. At medium speed, gradually beat in granulated sugar, 2 tablespoons at a time, beating after each addition. Continue to beat, occasionally cleaning side of bowl with rubber scraper, until mixture is thick and smooth—about 10 minutes.

4. Add flour mixture and lemon peel to egg mixture; with a wooden spoon, mix until smooth.

5. Refrigerate dough, covered, overnight. Also, refrigerate springerle rolling pin (see note).

6. Next day, lightly grease several large cookie sheets; sprinkle with anise seed.

7. Divide dough into 2 parts. Refrigerate until ready to roll out.

8. Sprinkle pastry cloth or wooden board lightly with confectioners' sugar.

9. Roll one part of dough on pastry cloth to coat with sugar; then roll out to an 8- by 5½-inch rectangle. Repeat with remaining dough.

10. Remove springerle pin from refrigerator. Coat lightly with confectioners' sugar. Starting from long side, slowly roll pin once, firmly and evenly, over dough, to make designs. (If dough sticks to springerle pin, peel off with a spatula.)

11. With floured sharp knife, carefully cut along straight lines in dough to make individual cookies.

12. With wide spatula, transfer cookies to prepared cookie sheets, placing them ½ inch apart.   Let stand, uncovered, at room temperature overnight.

13. Next day, preheat oven to 325°F.   Bake cookies 15 minutes, or just until light golden.   Remove to wire rack; cool completely.

14. Store Springerle in tightly covered container in a cool, dry place 1 to 2 weeks.

Makes about 2¼ dozen.

Note: A traditional springerle rolling pin can be found in German specialty stores and in some department stores.   The wooden pin is carved into several intricate molds, which leave their impression on the dough as it is rolled.

Index

Sauce (Continued)
  sweet-and-sour, smoked tongue with, 36
Sauerbraten, 30–31
  with gingersnaps, 31
Sauerkraut
  with apples, 26
  beef meatballs with, 32
  caraway, with pork, 47–48
  loin of pork with knackwurst, potatoes, and, 51
  and pork, 49–50
  pork goulash and, 48
  pork hocks and, 48–49
  and spareribs baked in cider, 52–53
Sausage, 53–56
  apple and cabbage casserole with, 55
  -and-apple meat loaf, 55–56
  bratwurst
    with paprika sauce, 53
    roast turkey with, 42
  frankfurter salad bowl, 54–55
  general data, 43
  hot potato salad with, 25
  kielbasa with red cabbage, 53–54
  knackwurst in beer, 54
  sweet-and-sour, 15
Schnitzel in Holstein sauce, 33–34
Sesame loaf cake, crusty, 71–72
Shrimp, pickled, 15
Soups, 12, 16–20
  cabbage, 16–17
  general data, 12
  green-pea, 18
  kraftbrühe mit frittaten, 16
  lentil, 17
    with ham, 17–18
  split-pea
    with ham, 18–19
    with knackwurst, 19
  yellow-pea, with pork, 20
Sour cream
  apple pancakes with topping of, 59–60
  pancakes with spicy applesauce, 60
  sauce, pork meatball casserole with, 51–52
Spareribs
  mustard, 14

  and sauerkraut baked in cider, 52–53
Split-pea soup
  with ham, 18–19
  with knackwurst, 19
Springerle, 87–88
Springerle rolling pin, 88
Stollen, 72–73
Strawberry(ies)
  Bavarian cream, strawberries on, 58–59
  in May wine bowl, 59
Streusel
  blueberry coffeecake, 74
  -layered coffeecake, 73–74
Strudel
  dough, 74–75
  fresh-cherry, 76–77
  general data, 62
  golden apple, 75–76
  warm cream-cheese, 77–78
Sweet-and-sour
  sauce, smoked tongue with, 36
  sausages, 15

Tongue, smoked beef
  with fruit sauce, 35–36
  with sweet-and-sour sauce, 36
Tortes
  chocolate-hazelnut, 66–67
  Linzer, 84–85
Turkey, roast, 41–42

Veal, 32–35
  general data, 27
  meatballs with caper sauce, 32–33
  pot pie, 34–35
  schnitzel in Holstein sauce, 33–34
Vegetables, 21–26
  general data, 8, 21
  See also names of vegetables

Walnuts, apple cake with, 63
Wines, 4–5, 9, 10–11

Yellow-pea soup with pork, 20